STAND OUT

Evidence-Based Learning for College and Career Readiness

4

THIRD EDITION

WORKBOOK

STACI JOHNSON

ROB JENKINS

Serge Ndalamba.

NATIONAL
GEOGRAPHIC
LEARNING

CENGAGE
Learning

Australia • Brazil • Mexico • Singapore • United Kingdom • United States

Stand Out 4: Evidence-Based Learning for College and Career Readiness, Third Edition
Staci Johnson and Rob Jenkins
Workbook

Publisher: Sherrise Roehr

Executive Editor: Sarah Kenney

Senior Development Editor: Margarita Matte

Assistant Editor: Patricia Giunta

Director of Global Marketing: Ian Martin

Executive Marketing Manager: Ben Rivera

Product Marketing Manager: Dalia Bravo

Media Researcher: Leila Hishmeh

Director of Content and Media Production:
   Michael Burggren

Production Manager: Daisy Sosa

Senior Print Buyer: Mary Beth Hennebury

Cover and Interior Designer:
   Brenda Carmichael

Composition: Lumina

Cover Image: Jade/Getty Images

Bottom Images: (Left to Right) Jay B Sauceda/
   Getty Images; Tripod/Getty Images;
   Portra Images/Getty Images; Portra Images/
   Getty Images; Mark Edward Atkinson/
   Tracey Lee/Getty Images; James Porter/Getty
   Images; Dear Blue/Getty Images; Seth Joel/
   Getty Images; LWA/Larry Williams/
   Getty Images; Dimitri Otis/Getty Images

For permission to use material from this text or product,
submit all requests online at **cengage.com/permissions**
Further permissions questions can be emailed to
permissionrequest@cengage.com

Work Book
ISBN 13: 978-1-305-65561-4

National Geographic Learning/Cengage Learning
20 Channel Center Street
Boston, MA 02210
USA

Cengage Learning is a leading provider of customized learning solutions with office locations around the globe, including Singapore, the United Kingdom, Australia, Mexico, Brazil and Japan. Locate our local office at:
international.cengage.com/region

Cengage Learning products are represented in Canada by Nelson Education, Ltd.

Visit National Geographic Learning online at **NGL.Cengage.com**
Visit our corporate website at **www.cengage.com**

Printed in the United States of America
Print Number: 02   Print Year: 2016

CONTENTS

PRE-UNIT: Welcome   **3**
LESSON 1   Fill out an admission application   3
LESSON 2   Identify learning strategies   6
LESSON 3   Write about your goals   9

UNIT 1: Balancing Your Life   **12**
LESSON 1   Compare past and present   12
LESSON 2   Determine goals   15
LESSON 3   Identify obstacles and give advice   18
LESSON 4   Write about an important person   21
LESSON 5   Identify and apply time-management skills   24
Unit 1 Practice Test   27

UNIT 2: Personal Finance   **28**
LESSON 1   Calculate expenses   28
LESSON 2   Identify ways to be a smart consumer   31
LESSON 3   Interpret credit card and loan information   34
LESSON 4   Analyze advertising techniques   37
LESSON 5   Write a business letter   40
Unit 2 Practice Test   43

UNIT 3: Housing   **44**
LESSON 1   Interpret housing advertisements   44
LESSON 2   Compare types of housing   47
LESSON 3   Identify housing preferences   50
LESSON 4   Identify the steps to buying a home   53
LESSON 5   Interpret mortgage information   56
Unit 3 Practice Test   59

UNIT 4: Community   **60**
LESSON 1   Locate community resources   60
LESSON 2   Use the telephone   63
LESSON 3   Give suggestions   66
LESSON 4   Interpret a road map   69
LESSON 5   Identify ways to volunteer in the community   72
Unit 4 Practice Test   75

UNIT 5: Health   76

LESSON 1   Identify health habits   76
LESSON 2   Describe symptoms   79
LESSON 3   Interpret doctor's instructions   82
LESSON 4   Interpret nutrition information   85
LESSON 5   Complete a health insurance form   88
Unit 5 Practice Test   91

UNIT 6: Getting Hired   92

LESSON 1   Identify skills and characteristics   92
LESSON 2   Conduct a job search   95
LESSON 3   Write a resume   98
LESSON 4   Write an e-mail   101
LESSON 5   Prepare for a job interview   104
Unit 6 Practice Test   107

UNIT 7: On the Job   108

LESSON 1   Identify different types of workplace behavior   108
LESSON 2   Identify workplace actions   111
LESSON 3   Communicate problems to a supervisor   114
LESSON 4   Make ethical decisions   117
LESSON 5   Ask for a raise   120
Unit 7 Practice Test   123

UNIT 8: Civic Responsibility   124

LESSON 1   Interpret civic responsibilities   124
LESSON 2   Apply for a driver's license and respond to a jury summons   127
LESSON 3   Communicate opinions about a community problem   130
LESSON 4   Interpret the electoral process   133
LESSON 5   Write and give a speech   136
Unit 8 Practice Test   139

APPENDICES   140

Glossary of grammar terms   140
Grammar reference   142
Photo credits   155
Map of the United States   156

TO THE TEACHER

ABOUT THE SERIES

The **Stand Out** series is designed to facilitate *active* learning within life-skill settings that leads students to career and academic pathways. Each student book and its supplemental components in the six-level series expose students to competency areas most useful and essential for newcomers, with careful treatment of level-appropriate but challenging materials. Students grow academically by developing essential literacy and critical thinking skills that will help them find personal success in a changing and dynamic world.

STAND OUT WORKBOOK

The **Stand Out Workbook** is designed to provide additional practice for learners to reinforce what they learned in each student book lesson. It can be used as homework or as a supplement to the lesson in the classroom. Each lesson in **Stand Out** is driven by a life-skill objective and supported by vocabulary and grammar. Students are not expected to master or acquire vocabulary and grammar completely after being exposed to it just one time, hence the need for additional practice. The lessons in the student book are three pages long and each supporting workbook lesson is also three pages long. The workbook lessons correlate directly with the student book lessons.

The **Stand Out Workbook** establishes a link to new content by providing the essential vocabulary introduced in the books in a way that also promotes critical thinking skills. Promoting critical thinking skills is essential for students to become independent lifelong learners. About half of the three-page practice is grammar focused where students are given a chart with notes, study how the grammar facilitates communication, and gain additional needed confidence through practice.

HOW TO USE THE STAND OUT WORKBOOK

The workbook can be used in the following ways:

1. The activities in the workbook can be used as additional practice during class to reinforce one or more practice activities in the student book.

2. The activities in the workbook can be assigned as homework. This is often a good way to reinforce what students have learned. The skills, vocabulary, and structures may not transfer into long-term memory after the lesson, so reinforcing the lesson after a short period of time away can be very helpful. Additionally, teachers can also review the homework at the beginning of each class, giving students another opportunity to be exposed to the information. Reviewing the homework is also a good strategy for the *Warm-up/Review* portion of the lesson and can be used in place of the one proposed in the **Stand Out Lesson Planner**.

3. The **Stand Out Workbook** can be used as a tool in the flipped classroom. In flipped classrooms, students prepare for lessons away from class before they are presented. Since the **Stand Out Workbook** introduces much of the vocabulary and grammar for each lesson, it is ideal for incorporating this approach.

ADDITIONAL PRACTICE

The **Stand Out** series is a comprehensive one-stop for all student needs. There is no need to look any further than the resources offered. Additional practice is available through the online workbook, which is different from the print workbook. There are also hundreds of multi-level worksheets available online. Please visit ngl.cengage.com/so3 to get easy access to all resources.

1 Tell me something about yourself

GOAL ■ Fill out an admission application

A. **What questions do you ask when you are meeting someone for the first time? Read and practice the following conversation.**

Elia: Hi, my name is Elia. What's your name?

Sandeep: I'm Sandeep. Nice to meet you.

Elia: Where are you from, Sandeep?

Sandeep: I'm from India. And you?

Elia: I'm from Spain. I've never been to India, but I've always wanted to go there.

Sandeep: Yes, it's a beautiful country. So, why are you studying English?

Elia: Well, all of my family is here. I came here to go to school so I could become a graphic designer.

Sandeep: Wow! That's ambitious.

Elia: What is your goal?

Sandeep: I just want to learn English so I can survive here.

Elia: Well, I want to do that, too, of course!

B. **What questions do Elia and Sandeep ask one another? Underline the questions and write them below.**

1. _____

2. _____

3. _____

4. _____

C. **How would you answer each of the questions above?**

1. _____

2. _____

3. _____

4. _____

D. **Study the charts.**

Information Questions (Present Tense)			
Question word	**Verb**	**Singular subject**	***You*/Plural subject**
What	is	your name? your goal?	
Who	is	your teacher?	
When	is	your class?	
Where	are		you from?
Why	*are*		you *studying* English?

Information Questions (Past Tense)			
Question word	**Verb**	**Singular subject**	***You*/Plural subject**
What	was	your goal?	
Who	was	your teacher?	
When	was	your class?	
Where	*were*		you *studying* English?
Why	*were*		you *living* there?

E. **Write the correct form of the *be* verb on the line.**

1. What _____ is _____ your name? (present)

2. Where _____ is _____ your class? (present)

3. What _____ is _____ your teacher's name? (past)

4. Why _____ are _____ they learning English? (present)

5. When _____ is _____ her class? (present)

6. What _____ was _____ his goal for this year? (past)

7. Who _____ is _____ your teacher? (present)

8. Where _____ was _____ your college? (past)

9. When _____ is _____ your class? (present)

F. **Write a question for each answer below.**

1. Q: What is your name?

   A: Jenni.

2. Q: Where way you?

   A: I was living at home to save money.

3. Q: what are you want to do

   A: I want to help my children with their homework.

4. Q: What's your mother, name

   A: Her name is Mrs. Wilhoit.

5. Q: Where are You from

   A: I'm from Ireland.

6. Q: When are you started to go to school.

   A: Last year, my class was on Saturdays.

7. Q: Where is your school.

   A: My school is near the library.

G. **Write a conversation like the one in exercise A. Include at least four questions.**

Student A: _____

Student B: _____

Student A: _____

Student B: _____

Student A: _____

Student B: _____

Student A: _____

Student B: _____

Student A: _____

Student B: _____

Student A: _____

Student B: _____

GOAL ■ Identify learning strategies

A. Read about Enrique.

> I'm trying to learn English, but I have really bad study habits. First of all, I study by myself so I get easily distracted. If there is something good on TV, I will turn the TV on while I'm studying. That's another problem—studying at home. I should probably study at the library or a coffee shop. And maybe if I studied with some of my classmates, I wouldn't find other things to do. Another problem is that I study late at night after work when I'm really tired. What should I do? I really want to be a good student, but it's hard sometimes.

B. Answer the questions about Enrique's study habits.

1. Where does Enrique study? _____

2. Who does he study with? _____

3. When does he study? _____

4. What does Enrique study? _____

C. What are Enrique's bad study habits? How could he improve his bad habits?

Bad habits	Ways to improve
1. study alone = easily distracted	
2.	
3.	

D. Study the chart.

Information Questions			
Question word	*Do* verb	Subject	Base verb
Who What Where When	do	I you we they	**study** with? **like** to read? **prefer** to study? **find** time to study?
Who What Where When	does	he she	**take** class with? **write** about? **meet** his classmates? **do** her homework?

E. Check (✓) the correct form of the verb *do*. Then, complete each question with a verb from the box and the correct form of *do*.

assign	prefer	like	write	meet	eat	want	study	take	~~buy~~

1. Where _____ we __buy__ our books?　　　　☑ do　　☐ does

2. Why _____ she _____ in the kitchen?　　☐ do　　☐ does

3. Who _____ your daughter _____ reading with?　☐ do　　☐ does

4. When _____ we _____ to meet to study?　☐ do　　☐ does

5. Where _____ she _____ to take classes?　☐ do　　☐ does

6. What _____ you _____ writing class or pronunciation class?　☐ do　　☐ does

7. How often _____ they _____ in their journals?　☐ do　　☐ does

8. When _____ your teacher _____ homework?　☐ do　　☐ does

9. Who _____ she _____ with?　　　　☐ do　　☐ does

10. Where _____ the study group _____?　☐ do　　☐ does

11. How often _____ he _____ to eat?　　☐ do　　☐ does

F. Write four questions to ask your classmates about their study habits.

1. _____

2. _____

3. _____

4. _____

G. Write answers for the questions in Exercise F.

Question	Answer
1.	
2.	
3.	
4.	

H. Imagine you work for the school newspaper and you are writing about an interview. Write your questions about study habits and the answers your classmate might have provided.

Q: _____

A: _____

Q: _____

A: _____

Q: _____

A: _____

Q: _____

A: _____

LESSON ③ What are your goals?

GOAL ■ Write about your goals

A. **There are seven mistakes in Giulia's paragraph. Circle each mistake you find.**

> I move to the United States from Italy three year ago with two goals
> in mind: to get a good education and start my own business. First,
> I need to improve my english so I can get into a good universty. Second,
> I need to study hard to get my degree. And finally, I will be able to open
> up my own travel agency. I know if I works hard very, my dreams will
> come true

B. **Complete the table with the mistakes and the corrections.**

Mistake	Correction
move	moved

C. Read the chart on editing.

Editing		
Term	**Rule**	**Examples**
Capitalization	Every sentence and proper noun should begin with a capital letter.	<u>S</u>he loves her hometown. Giulia studies <u>E</u>nglish.
Spelling	Every word should be spelled correctly.	**<u>university</u>**
Nouns	Every noun should be in the correct singular or plural form.	Giulia has two **<u>goals</u>**. (not *goal*) They have five **<u>children</u>**. (not *childrens*)
Verbs	Every verb should be in the correct tense and agree with the noun.	She **<u>moved</u>** three years ago. She **<u>is</u>** a student.
Word order	Words should be in the correct order.	She wants to get a **<u>good education</u>**. (not *education good*)
Punctuation	Every sentence should end with a period, question mark, or exclamation point.	Giulia wants her own business**<u>.</u>** Where do you study**<u>?</u>**

D. Each sentence has one mistake. Decide if the mistake is *capitalization, spelling, noun, verb agreement, word order,* or *punctuation* and write it on the line. Then, correct the mistake.

1. A dental technician clean teeth. _____ *cleans / verb* _____

2. My goals is to become a dental technician. _____

3. It will probably take me at least five years because there are steps many I need

   to take. _____

4. first, I need to find a good school to get my certificate from. _____

5. Then, I need to take and pass all the required Classes. _____

6. After that, I have to find an internship so I can get some on-the-job

   traning. _____

7. Once I have my certificate and training, I can look for a job _____

8. Hopefully, it won't takes too long! _____

E. Read the paragraph and find each mistake. Then, complete the information in the table.

ever since I can remember, I has wanted to be a computer programmer. My ideal job is to work for a gaming company, creating new video game. first, I want to go to school so I can make sure my skills are as good as they need to be Second, I need to come up with some good new idea that I can present to a company when I interveiw. Then, I need to send my resume to several company. Hopefully, they'll likes me and my work when we meet and give me the job.

Term	Mistake	Correction
1. capitalization	ever	Ever
2.		
3.		
4.		
5.		
6.		
7.		
8.		
9.		

F. Write a paragraph about your goals.

_____

_____

_____

_____

_____

_____

_____

_____

G. Go back and look for mistakes in your paragraph. Underline each one you find and then fix it.

LESSON **1** **Where did you use to study?**

GOAL ■ Compare past and present

A. Categorize the phrases in the box in the columns below.

next week	last year	tomorrow	today
two years ago	tonight	right now	yesterday

PAST   PRESENT   FUTURE

_____   _____   _____

_____   _____   _____

_____   _____   _____

B. Diego wrote down some things that he did in the past and things that he does now. Look at his chart.

PAST	NOW
studied by myself	study with friends
took English classes	take computer classes
exercised in the morning	exercise in the evening

C. Complete the sentences below. Use the information in the chart.

1. Diego used to study by himself, but now he studies with _____.

2. Diego used to take _____ classes, but now he takes _____ classes.

3. He used to _____ in the _____, but now he _____ at night.

4. Diego's friend, Mark, will normally _____ in the evening, but after he decided

   to _____ with friends, he went back to his former routine when he used to

   _____ in the morning.

D. Study the chart.

Used to	
Example	**Rule**
Diego *used to* <u>study</u> by himself. He *used to* <u>take</u> English classes.	**Affirmative:** *used to* + base verb
Diego *did not use to* <u>study</u> with friends. He *didn't use to* <u>exercise</u> at night.	**Negative:** *did + not (didn't) + use to* + base verb **Incorrect:** ~~I didn't used to go to school.~~
Use ***used to*** + base verb to talk about a past habit or custom that was true for a period of time in the past, but is not true now.	

E. Complete the sentences below. Fill in one blank with *used to/didn't use to* + base verb. Fill in the other blank with the simple present.

1. Mr. Ray _____*used to build*_____ (build) homes, but now he _____*teaches*_____ (teach) English.

2. Tara _____ (not go) to school, but now she _____ (attend) school full-time.

3. I _____ (spend) a lot of money, but now I _____ (save) my money.

4. Now we _____ (live) in a house, but we _____ (rent) an apartment.

5. You _____ (not speak) English, but now you _____ (speak) well.

6. Now I _____ (assemble) computers, but I _____ (not work).

7. I _____ (run) in the mornings, but now I _____ (play) volleyball at night.

F. Write sentences about what the people *used to/didn't use to* do.

1. my brother / not / live in Caracas   <u>My brother didn't use to live in Caracas.</u>

2. Maya / drive to work   _____

3. you / not / save money   _____

4. I / not / have time for my family   _____

5. Teresa / have a different job   _____

6. we / attend school at night   _____

7. they / plan everything in advance   _____

8. Don / not / have a lot of patience   _____

9. I / focus on the important things in life   _____

G. Complete the chart below with things you used to do in the past compared to things you do now.

Used to do	Do now
1.	1.
2.	2.
3.	3.

H. Write three sentences about things you used to do, but that you don't do now. Use information from the chart in Exercise G.

1. _____

2. _____

3. _____

LESSON **2** Reaching your goals

GOAL ■ Determine goals

A. **A synonym is a word with a similar meaning. Match each word to the correct synonym.**

1. architect
2. design
3. graduate
4. license
5. retired

a. create
b. finish
c. elderly
d. certificate
e. designer

B. **Read about Bita and Minh.**

Bita used to live in Iran, but now she lives in the United States. She moved to the United States to get a better education. She used to be an architect designing schools and hospitals. She would like to do the same thing in the United States, but she needs to improve her English and get her license.

Minh came to the United States from Vietnam, where he used to work for a computer company. Also, he used to make jewelry, which he learned how to do from his father. Now, he is retired and helps take care of his grandchildren. Someday, he hopes to see them graduate from college.

C. **Answer the questions about Bita and Minh.**

1. Where did they use to live? _____

2. Did Bita use to work for a computer company? _____

3. Did Minh use to make jewelry? _____

4. What did Bita use to do for work? _____

5. What is Minh's goal? _____

6. What is Bita's goal? _____

D. Study the chart.

Use to and Used to in Questions		
	Example	**Rule**
Yes/No Questions	**Did** Minh **use to** work? **Did** Bita **use to** study English?	**Yes/No question:** *did* + subject + *use to* + base verb
Wh- Questions (*where, when, why*)	Where **did** Minh **use to** work? When **did** Bita **use to** study? Why **did** Minh **use to** make jewelry?	**Wh- question:** *wh-* word + *did* + subject + *use to* + base verb
Wh- Questions (*who, what*)	*Who **used to** live in Iran? What **did** Minh **use to** do in Vietnam?	**Wh- question:** *wh-* word + *did* + subject + *use to* + base verb
• Most *Yes/No* and *Wh-* questions omit the *d* in *used to*.		

E. Write *Yes/No* questions with *use to*. Use the words from the chart.

1. you / work part-time /   <u>Did you use to work part-time?</u>

2. he / live with his family   _____

3. Lin / have time for friends   _____

4. you / drive to work   _____

5. they / feel hopeful   _____

6. Yuri / exercise   _____

7. they / plan in advance   _____

8. she / be a librarian   _____

9. we / own a restaurant   _____

F. Write *Wh-* questions with *use to*. Ask about the underlined portion of each answer.

1. **Q:** <u>Who used to assemble computers?</u>

   A: <u>Mario</u> used to assemble computers.

2. **Q:** _____

   A: I used to work <u>every day</u>.

3. **Q:** _____

   A: She used to take the bus <u>because she couldn't drive</u>.

4. **Q:** _____

   A: We used to make <u>jewelry</u>.

5. Q: _____

    A: I used to attend classes <u>at Glen Community College</u>.

6. Q: _____

    A: They used to study <u>at night</u>.

7. Q: _____

    A: Bita used to live with <u>her family</u>.

G. Write four *Yes/No* and *Wh-* questions. Then, write the answers in complete sentences.

1. Q: Where did you use to study? _____

    A: I used to study at Bellingham Adult School. _____

2. Q: _____

    A: _____

3. Q: _____

    A: _____

4. Q: _____

    A: _____

5. Q: _____

    A: _____

H. Think about goals that you had in the past and write three sentences about those goals using *used to*.

1. I used to want to own my own clothing store. I used to want to work in a bank.

2. _____

3. _____

4. _____

I. Write questions that someone might ask you with *use to*.

1. Did you use to work in a clothing store? _____

2. _____

3. _____

4. _____

LESSON ③ What should I do?

GOAL ■ Identify obstacles and give advice

A. Define the following in your own words.

1. A *goal* is _____.

2. An *obstacle* is _____.

3. A *solution* is _____.

4. *Advice* is _____.

B. Complete the chart below with possible solutions.

Name	Goal	Obstacle	Possible solutions
Amir	get a job	doesn't speak good enough English	1. take English classes 2.
Bell family	buy a house	don't have enough money	1. 2.
Claudia	be a stay-at-home mom	needs to make money to help with the bills	1. 2.

C. Share your ideas with other students. Did you come up with the same or different solutions?

D. Study the chart.

Be + Infinitive		
Modal / Expression	**Example**	**Rule**
could	Amir **could** *take* English classes.	*could* + base verb
should	Claudia **should** *work* part-time at night.	*should* + base verb
How about …	**How about** *going* to school?	*How about* + gerund
Why don't you … Why doesn't he/she … Why don't they …	**Why don't you** *move* to a different city? **Why doesn't he** *practice* English with his children? **Why don't they** *save* money for a few years?	*Why don't/doesn't* + subject + base verb

**E. Complete each sentence. Use modals and expressions: *could, should, How about …,*
or *Why don't …?***

1. _____Why don't they_____ put the two kids in one room?

2. They _____ move into a bigger house.

3. _____ finding a different teacher?

4. _____ ask your boss for a raise?

5. Elia _____ buy a new computer.

6. _____ walking to work?

7. We _____ do the household chores together.

8. _____ look for a part-time job at night?

9. _____ doing your homework before the kids
   wake up in the morning?

10. _____ find a different school, one that is closer
    to his job?

11. You _____ find some friends to study with.

F. Complete each piece of advice with the correct form of a verb from the box.

finish	ask	wait	work
tell	fix	paint	study

1. Why don't you _____ the car yourself?

2. How about _____ your brother for help?

3. Luther could _____ the inside of the house and hire someone to paint the outside.

4. Why don't you _____ your mother you don't need her help?

5. Cade should _____ school before he gets a full-time job.

6. How about _____ for a new class to start?

7. Why don't they _____ when they get home from school?

8. Erika could _____ from home so she can be there for her kids.

G. Look at the possible solutions you wrote in Exercise B. Write sentences giving advice. Use the new expressions you learned.

1. _How about taking some English classes?_____

2. _____

3. _____

4. _____

5. _____

6. _____

GOAL ■ Write about an important person

A. Read Gary's paragraph about his teacher.

> The teacher who influenced me the most in my life is Mrs. Hargrove. She was my English teacher when I first came here from South Africa, and she taught at the school where my brother went. She influenced me the most because she showed me how important it is to get a college education. I've always wanted to be a computer programmer, so now I am studying at a local community college. When I finished her class, Mrs. Hargrove gave me a book that always reminds me of her.

B. Underline the following words in the paragraph in Exercise A. Define them in your own words.

1. influenced: _____

2. computer programmer: _____

3. reminds: _____

C. Answer the questions.

1. Who influenced Gary? _____

2. What school did Mrs. Hargrove teach at? _____

3. What is special about the book that Mrs. Hargrove gave Gary? _____

D. Read the conversation.

Gary: I want to get a present for Mrs. Hargrove to thank her for all her help.

Elisa: Is she the teacher that gave you the book?

Gary: Yes. She is the first teacher I had when I came here. And now that I've gotten into college, I know she will be so proud.

Elisa: I'm sure that she knows how hard you worked.

Gary: She does. But I still want to get her something nice that will remind her how important she is to students like me.

E. What do you think would be a good gift for Gary to give to Mrs. Hargrove?

F.   Study the chart.

	Adjective Clauses
Person	The teacher **who** influenced me the most in my life is Mrs. Hargrove. (The teacher is Mrs. Hargrove. **She** influenced me the most in my life.)
Place	She taught at the school **where** my brother went. (She taught at the school. My brother went **there**.)
Thing	Mrs. Hargrove gave me a book **that** always reminds me of her. (Mrs. Hargrove gave me a book. **It** always reminds me of her.)

- An adjective clause is a group of words that describe the preceding noun (either a subject noun or an object noun).
- *Who, where,* and *that* are relative pronouns that begin adjective clauses. Relative pronouns replace the subject or object. (See bold words above.)
- All adjective clauses contain a noun and a verb and express an incomplete thought.

G.   Read the following sentences. Underline the adjective clause and circle the noun that it describes.

1. I'm in a study (group) that likes to meet at night.

2. The book that we use in class is interesting.

3. She studies in a place where it is very quiet.

4. They practice speaking with their neighbors who are native English speakers.

5. The man who sits in front of me is very good at grammar.

6. Enrique takes classes that give him a lot of homework.

7. The school where Anna studies is close to her home.

H.   Write the correct relative pronoun (*that, who, where*) to begin each adjective clause.

1. He is the professor _____ convinced me to go to college.

2. Do you know of a school _____ has computer classes?

3. I study at a library _____ there are private study rooms.

4. Kenji takes a writing class from a teacher _____ is from Serbia.

I. **Read about omitting the relative pronoun.**

Omission of the Relative Pronoun in Adjective Clauses

The relative pronoun can be omitted from the adjective clause if there is a <u>subject</u> following the **relative pronoun**. Look at the examples below:
    The book (**that**) <u>she</u> gave me sits on the shelf above my desk.
    She is the teacher (**who/whom***) <u>I</u> told you about.
    She is the first teacher (**that**) <u>I</u> had when I came here.

*****Who** is more common in everyday conversation. **Whom** is used in more formal situations.

J. **Rewrite these sentences without the relative pronoun.**

1. The book (**that**) she gave me sits on the shelf above my desk.

   The book she gave me sits on the shelf above my desk.

2. She is the teacher (**who/whom**) <u>I</u> told you about.

   _____

3. She is the first teacher (**that**) <u>I</u> had when I came here.

   _____

4. I'm sure (**that**) <u>she</u> knows how hard you worked.

   _____

K. **Decide if the relative pronoun in each sentence can be omitted. If so, cross it out.**

1. Trinh's family is very proud of the obstacles ~~that~~ he has overcome.
2. The dreams that he had for the future are now a reality.
3. He is going to attend the college that was his first choice.
4. In high school, Trinh had a teacher that he often went to see for advice.
5. Mrs. Jones was the kind of person that always made time for her students.

L. **Complete each sentence with information from your life. Then, combine the sentences using an adjective clause.**

1. *Sacramento* _____ is a city. I grew up there.

   Sacramento is the city where I grew up. _____

2. _____ is a teacher. She/He taught me how to read.

   _____

3. _____ is a place. I like to study there.

   _____

4. This is a _____. _____ gave it to me.

   _____

LESSON **5** Time management

GOAL ■ Identify and apply time-management skills

A. Read the list of time-management strategies. Check (✓) the box next to each strategy you follow. Then, check whether that strategy is a good or bad one.

	Strategy	Good	Bad
☐	Prioritize your tasks	☐	☐
☐	Plan far in advance	☐	☐
☐	Leave things until the last minute	☐	☐
☐	Forget appointments	☐	☐
☐	Ask people for help	☐	☐
☐	Do two things at once	☐	☐
☐	Get burned out	☐	☐
☐	Make a list of your tasks	☐	☐

B. Complete each sentence with words from the box.

accomplish	achievements	allocate	simultaneously	sacrifices
importance	prioritize	realistic	deadlines	strategies

1. Time-management _____ can help you _____ your goals.

2. When keeping a schedule, you need to _____ time slots to each task.

3. Sometimes you need to make _____ in order to get everything done.

4. Be _____ about how much time it takes to complete each task.

5. If you have a lot of things to get done in one day, _____ them in order of

_____ .

6. It will help if you can do two things _____ .

7. It is important to set _____ so that things get done on time.

8. Having a positive attitude about time management will help you appreciate your

_____ .

C. Study the chart.

Expressions for Suggestions, Advice, and Necessity		
Modal	Example	**Meaning**
could	You **could** plan far in advance.	suggestion
should **shouldn't**	They **should** wake up earlier in the morning. They **shouldn't** stay up too late.	advice
have to **not have to**	He **has to** keep a schedule. He **doesn't have to** worry so much.	necessity
need to **not need to**	I **need to** remember what is important in life. I **don't need to** sacrifice my health.	necessity

- *Could* and *should* are modals. Always use a base verb after a modal.
- *Have to* and *need to* are expressions that are like modals in meaning. Add *-s* to these expressions in the third-person singular.

D. Unscramble the words to write sentences with modals.

1. needs to / a list of tasks / Juan / make   _Juan needs to make a list of tasks._

2. do / two tasks / should / simultaneously / he   _____

3. plan / I / in advance / have to   _____

4. to the last minute / I / leave things / shouldn't   _____

5. you / your best / do / need to   _____

6. have / could / you / more patience   _____

7. sacrifice / shouldn't / we / time with friends   _____

8. get burned out / don't have to / we   _____

9. we / everything / accomplish / don't need to   _____

E. Answer each question using the word in parentheses.

1. Should I get a new job? (yes)   _Yes, you should get a new job._

2. Does she need to save money? (no)   _____

3. Could you buy a used car? (yes)   _____

4. Shouldn't he get more training? (yes)   _____

5. Do I have to take more courses? (no)   _____

6. Should we move closer to work? (yes)   _____

7. Don't you have to leave your job? (no)   _____

8. Should she ask someone for help? (yes)   _____

9. Doesn't he need to manage his time? (yes)   _____

F. **Read about each person's problem with time. Suggest two strategies to help. Use *could*, *should*, *have to*, or *need to*.**

1. Eva has a lot of doctor's appointments for herself and her three children. She can never remember when they are and she often misses them.

   a. _____

   b. _____

2. Franco is so busy with work and school that he can never find time to visit his family and friends.

   a. _____

   b. _____

3. Ari has so many things to do in one day that he often forgets what he needs to do and what he has already done.

   a. _____

   b. _____

4. Kenji works during the day and goes to school at night. His doctor told him he needs to start exercising, but he doesn't have the time.

   a. _____

   b. _____

G. **Write a short paragraph about what you would like to do differently in your life related to time management. Try to use some of the new vocabulary words from Exercise B.**

_____

_____

_____

_____

_____

_____

_____

PRACTICE TEST

A. Look at the chart and choose the best answer.

Name	Goal	Obstacle
Shelby	become a surgical nurse	doesn't speak good enough English
Sanjay & Farrah	buy a house	don't have enough money
Antonio	work from home	no other employees at his company work from home

1. Who wants to change his or her position at work?
   - a. Shelby
   - b. Sanjay
   - c. Farrah
   - d. Antonio

2. What does Shelby need to do if she wants to become a surgical nurse?
   - a. make some more money to pay for school
   - b. improve her English
   - c. work from home
   - d. go to nursing school

3. What does Antonio need to do if he wants to work from home?
   - a. look for another job
   - b. convince his boss that he will be productive at home
   - c. both a and b
   - d. none of the above

4. Sanjay and his wife don't have enough money to do what?
   - a. work from home
   - b. move to another city
   - c. change jobs
   - d. buy a house

5. Who needs to go to school and take English classes?
   - a. Shelby
   - b. Sanjay
   - c. Farrah
   - d. Antonio

LESSON 1 Money in, money out

GOAL ■ Calculate expenses

A. Think about the following terms related to budgeting. Describe them in your own words.

1. monthly expenses: _____

2. budgeted amount: _____

3. actual amount spent: _____

B. Look at George and Judy's budget and answer the questions that follow.

Monthly Expenses for June	Budgeted Amount	Actual Amount Spent
Auto (loan, gas, repairs)	$1,100	$995
Phone (home and mobile)	$110	$127.43
Satellite	$45	$45
Internet	$39.95	$39.95
Entertainment	$100	$140
Groceries	$250	$180
Medical	$300	$0
Mortgage	$2,200	$2,200
Retirement	$400	$400
Utilities (gas, electricity, water)	$125	$150
TOTAL		

1. What are the totals for Budgeted Amount and Actual Amount Spent? Write the totals in the chart.

2. How much did they budget for entertainment? _____

3. How much did they budget for groceries? _____

4. Which exceeds the budget more, phone or medical? _____

C. Study the chart.

How much	
Examples	**Rule**
How much *do* **you** *spend* on school? How much *does* **she** *budget* for entertainment?	Simple present *do/does* + **subject** + *base verb*
How much *did* **he** *budget* for his mortgage? How much *did* **she** *save* for retirement?	Simple past *did* + **subject** + *base verb*
How much *is* **he** *spending* on electricity? How much *are* **they** *saving* for college?	Present continuous *am/is/are* + **subject** + *-ing verb*

D. Check (✓) the correct response for each question.

1. How much _____ for entertainment?   ☑ do they budget   ☐ does they budget

2. How much _____ on dining out each week?   ☐ do you spend   ☐ do you spending

3. How much _____ for new clothes?   ☐ is she save   ☐ is she saving

4. How much _____ on photography supplies?   ☐ did she spend   ☐ did she spends

5. How much _____ on travel last year?   ☐ did they spend   ☐ are they spending

6. How much _____ for his cell phone?   ☐ does he budget   ☐ do he budget

7. How much _____ for books for school?   ☐ did I pay   ☐ did I paid

8. How much _____ for your mother's hospital bills?   ☐ are you save   ☐ are you saving

9. How much _____ for their daughter's college fund?   ☐ are they putting away   ☐ is they putting away

10. How much _____ for our vacation next summer?   ☐ do you have   ☐ are you have

11. How much _____ from the bank each week?   ☐ does he get   ☐ do he get

E. Complete each sentence with the correct form of the verb in parentheses.

Present Tense

1. (pay) How much _____do_____ we _____pay_____ for our Internet?

2. (spend) How much _____ Eric usually _____ on groceries each month?

3. (pay) How much _____ we _____ for our house?

Past Tense

4. (budget) How much _____ you _____ for utilities?

5. (save) How much _____ their family _____ for vacations?

Present Continuous

6. (pay) How much _____ I _____ for my school registration?

7. (budget) How much _____ she _____ for car repairs?

Your Choice

8. (spend) How much _____ our classmates _____ on entertainment?

9. (save) How much _____ my mother _____ for medical expenses?

F. Write three *How much* questions to ask your partner.

1. _____

2. _____

3. _____

G. Write what you think your partner's answers would be in complete sentences.

1. _____

2. _____

3. _____

LESSON **2** Savvy shopper

GOAL ■ Identify ways to be a smart consumer

A. Imagine you are trying to help a family member make a large purchase. What is the most important thing you would tell them about each topic listed below?

1. Budget: _____

2. Shop around: _____

3. Read sales ads carefully: _____

4. Carefully consider bargain offers: _____

   _____

5. Ask about return policies: _____

   _____

6. Ask about warranties: _____

   _____

B. Answer the questions about yourself with short answers.

1. What would you buy if you had an extra $5,000?   _____

2. If you had to move, where would you live?   _____

3. If you could change jobs, what would you be?   _____

4. If you didn't work or go to school, what would you do?   _____

5. If you won the lottery, what is the first thing you would do?   _____

6. If you could change anything in the world, what would it be?   _____

7. If you dyed your hair, what color would it be?   _____

8. What movie would you like to see if you had the time?   _____

C. Study the chart.

Contrary-to-Fact Conditionals: Statements	
Condition (*if* + subject + past tense verb)	**Result** (subject + *would* + base verb)
If I had a million dollars, **If you didn't have** so much work, **If she were** a smart consumer, **If I weren't** busy,	**I would buy** a new house. **you would take** a long vacation. **she would read** sales ads carefully. **I would shop** around.

- A contrary-to-fact statement is a sentence that is not true at this point in time.
- A comma is used between the two clauses when the *if* clause comes first.
- The *if* clause can come first or second. When it comes second, no comma is used.
  I would buy a new house **if I had** a million dollars.
- In the *if* clause, use *were* instead of *was* with *I, he, she,* and *it.*

D. Circle the condition. Underline the result.

1. <u>I would buy</u> a new house (if I earned) enough for the mortgage payments.

2. If he had a credit card, he would charge all his purchases.

3. I would buy a new car if I saved more money.

4. If she weren't so busy, she would do more research on the Internet.

5. If I didn't need more money, I would retire next year.

6. You would have money for all your monthly expenses if you adjusted your budget.

7. If he were a smart consumer, he would go online to make his purchases.

8. If you read the return policy, you would see that you cannot get a full refund.

9. We would have extra money if we didn't travel so much.

10. They would move to a larger house if there were larger houses in their neighborhood.

11. If Mrs. Bell didn't have such high medical bills, she would contribute more to her 401K.

E. Unscramble the conditions. Write a result.

1. made / if / more money / I   If I made more money, I would buy a boat.

2. if / had / I / a better job   _____

3. lived / if / in a nicer house / I   _____

4. a raise at work / I / got / if   _____

F. Complete each sentence with the correct form of the verbs in parentheses.

1. If Maya _____went_____ (go) to technical school, she _____would get_____ (get) a better job.

2. She _____ (save) a lot of money if she _____ (be) careful with her finances.

3. If she _____ (not work) so much, she _____ (have) more time to relax.

4. Her husband Marco _____ (buy) a new computer if he _____ (need) one.

5. If they _____ (read) the sales ads carefully, they _____ (find) a good bargain.

6. If I _____ (be) Maya, I _____ (shop) around.

7. If we _____ (not be) so busy, we _____ (compare) more prices.

8. Marco _____ (give) money to charity if he _____ (not / have) so many expenses.

9. If you _____ (have) extra money, you _____ (give) money to charity, too.

10. Marco and Maya _____ (take) a vacation if they _____ (not spend) so much money on their rent.

11. If they _____ (win) the lottery, they _____ (retire) and travel.

G. Look back at the questions in Exercise B. Write complete conditional statements that include your answers.

1. If I had an extra $5,000, I would buy a new computer. _____

2. _____

3. _____

4. _____

5. _____

H. Look back at the questions in Exercise B. Write complete conditional statements about what a family member or friend would answer.

1. If Jessica could change jobs, she would be a veterinarian. _____

2. _____

3. _____

4. _____

5. _____

LESSON ③ Charge it!

GOAL ■ Interpret credit card and loan information

A. Think about the pros and cons of using a credit card. Brainstorm your ideas below. Use some of the words from the box in your lists.

APR	grace period	annual fee
cash back	discounts	credit limit

USING A CREDIT CARD

Pros	Cons

B. Answer the questions about yourself. Circle *Yes* or *No*.

1. If you had more money, would you buy a new car?	Yes	No
2. If you won the lottery, would you buy a new house?	Yes	No
3. If you could pay off your mortgage, would you?	Yes	No
4. If you could have ten credit cards, would you?	Yes	No

C. Now, ask your partner the questions below. Circle his or her answers.

1. If you had more money, would you buy a small business?	Yes	No
2. If you were a millionaire, would you own more than one house?	Yes	No
3. If you had more time to go to school, would you get a master's degree?	Yes	No
4. If you could have any job in the world, would you want to be a doctor?	Yes	No

D. Study the chart.

Contrary-to-Fact Conditionals: *Yes/No* Questions		
If + subject + past tense / *would* + subject + base verb	**Short answer**	
If you had more money, **would you buy** a car? **If he didn't have** so much work, **would he take** a vacation? **If they weren't** busy, **would they shop** around?	Yes, I **would.** Yes, he **would.** Yes, they **would.**	No, I **wouldn't.** No, he **wouldn't.** No, they **wouldn't.**
• A *Yes/No* question in a contrary-to-fact conditional is formed in the result clause. • The *if* clause can come first or second. When it comes second, no comma is used. Would you buy a car **if you had** more money?		

E. Write a question using each statement.

1. If you got a raise, you would have extra money for entertainment.

   If you got a raise, would you have extra money for entertainment?

2. If he didn't spend so much money on rent, he would give more money to charity.

   _____

3. Martina would travel more if she weren't so busy.

   _____

4. If we had more time to relax, we would visit friends and family.

   _____

5. If I calculated my expenses, I would be able to adjust my budget.

   _____

F. Complete each sentence using the words given. Then, use *yes* or *no* to answer.

1. (buy new furniture) If you had a bigger apartment, *would you buy new furniture* _____?

   (no) *No, I wouldn't.* _____

2. (get approved for a loan) If he didn't owe so much money, _____?

   (yes) _____

3. (be persuaded to buy it) If you saw a special offer for a new car, _____?

   (no) _____

G. Imagine you are talking to a credit card company representative on the phone. Write four *Yes/No* questions you might ask him or her.

1. If I wanted to transfer balances from another credit card, would there be a fee?

2. _____

_____

3. _____

_____

4. _____

_____

5. _____

_____

H. Imagine you are getting a loan to start a small business. Write four *Yes/No* questions you might ask.

1. If I wanted to pay off my loan early, would there be a penalty?

2. _____

_____

3. _____

_____

4. _____

_____

5. _____

_____

LESSON **4** How they pull you in

GOAL ■ Analyze advertising techniques

A. Read the advertisement for Grandma's Cookies. Would you buy these cookies? Why or why not?

Grandma's Cookies

Our cookies are made with ALL natural ingredients.

NOTHING BUT THE BEST!

Oatmeal Raisin *is made with real raisins!*
Chocolate Chip *is made with dark chocolate!*
Peanut Butter Chunk *is made with actual chunks of peanut butter!*

Grandma's Cookies are sold at health-food markets.

B. Answer the questions.

1. What is being advertised? _____

2. What does the ad say to persuade you to buy the cookies?

    _____

3. Where can you buy these cookies? _____

4. What do you think makes these cookies different from other cookies?

    _____

C. Study the chart.

Passive Voice: Present	
Example	**Explanation**
Cookies *are* **made** with natural ingredients.	*be* + **past participle**
The cookies *are* **sold** at health-food markets.	
• Use the passive voice to emphasize the object of the action or when the doer of the action is unknown or unimportant.	

D. Review the past particles by completing the table.

Base Verb	Past Participle	Base Verb	Past Participle
1. bring	brought	2. feel	
3. give		4. know	
5. hold		6. make	
7. sell		8. tell	
9. write		10. think	

E. Check (✓) the correct response next to each statement.

1. Many products _____ because of ads.
   ☐ is sold   ☑ are sold

2. Ads _____ in magazines, newspapers, on television, and a variety of other places.
   ☐ are place   ☐ are placed

3. Today, many ads _____ on the Internet.
   ☐ is found   ☐ are found

4. A product _____ often _____ through a pop-up ad.
   ☐ are advertised   ☐ is advertised

5. A pop-up ad on the Internet _____ to sell products.
   ☐ are used   ☐ is used

6. Sometimes, pop-up ads _____ by individual computers.
   ☐ is blocked   ☐ are blocked

7. A pop-up ad _____ by the user of the computer.
   ☐ is click on   ☐ is clicked on

8. Your information _____ by websites that you regularly go to.
   ☐ is stored   ☐ are stored

9. That information _____ by companies who want you to buy their products.
   ☐ are bought   ☐ is bought

F. **Complete each sentence with the passive voice using the correct form of the verb in parentheses.**

1. Coupons ___are put___ (put) in ads to entice readers to take an action.

2. Graphic artists _____ (hire) to create logos and artwork for advertisements.

3. Ads _____ (create) to make consumers aware of products.

4. Today, many products _____ (sell) over the Internet.

5. Consumers _____ (convince) to buy products by creative advertising.

6. Sometimes, consumers _____ (trick) by ads.

7. Special offers _____ (use) to sell more products.

8. Products _____ (buy) by consumers.

9. Sometimes, consumers _____ (convince) by ads.

G. **Imagine you are writing an ad for television. Write sentences for your ad in the passive voice using the verbs in parentheses.**

1. (do) _Warranty repairs are done on-site._____

2. (sell) _____

3. (make) _____

4. (find) _____

5. (fix) _____

6. (refund) _____

7. (answer) _____

H. **Think about a print ad for the television ad you wrote in Exercise G. Sketch your ad below.**

GOAL ■ Write a business letter

A. Answer the following questions about yourself.

1. If you didn't like your food in a restaurant, what would you do?

   I would _____.

2. If you wanted to dispute a charge on your credit card bill, whom would you call?

   I would _____.

3. If you received bad customer service in a store, what would you do?

   I would _____.

4. If you ordered something on the Internet and it never came, what would you do?

   I would _____.

B. Think about a family member or a friend. What would they say?

1. If he/she didn't like the food in a restaurant, what would he/she do?

   He/She would _____.

2. If he/she wanted to dispute a charge on a credit card bill, whom would he/she call?

   He/She would _____.

3. If he/she received bad customer service in a store, what would he/she do?

   He/She would _____.

4. If he/she ordered something on the Internet and it never came, what would he/she do?

   He/She would _____.

C. Write about an experience when you returned something, disputed a charge, or sent something back at a restaurant. What did you do? How did the person respond?

_____

_____

_____

_____

_____

D. Study the chart.

Contrary-to-Fact Conditionals: *Wh-* Questions	
Question	**Answer**
If + subject + past tense, *wh-* word + *would* + subject + base verb	Subject + *would* + base verb
If you received a bad meal, what would you do?	I would speak to the manager.
If a clerk yelled at him, how would he react?	He would calmly walk out of the store.
If her computer stopped working, whom would she call?	She would call the store where she bought it.
• A *wh-* question in a contrary-to-fact conditional is formed in the result clause. • The *if* clauses can come first or second. When it comes second, no comma is used. *What would you do if you received a bad meal?*	

E. Complete each sentence with the correct form of the verbs in parentheses.

1. If she ___slipped and fell___ (slip / fall) in the market, what ___would she do___ (do)?

2. If you _____ (not / like) the service, whom _____ (talk) to?

3. If his camera _____ (stop) working, what _____ (do)?

4. Why _____ (return) the books if you already _____ (read) them?

5. If you _____ (complain) about the service, what _____ (expect) the manager to do?

6. If we _____ (wrote) a letter to complain, where _____ (send) it?

7. If they _____ (receive) a broken TV, where _____ (take) it back to?

8. Where _____ (find) the supervisor if I _____ to talk to him?

9. If our family _____ (have) a bad experience on the plane, what

   _____ (do)?

F. **Complete the *wh-* question for the underlined portion of each answer.**

1. **Q:** If I didn't like a product I bought, <u>what would I have to write</u> _____ ?
   A: You would have to write <u>a letter of complaint</u>.

2. **Q:** If I didn't know the address of the company, _____ ?
   A: You would find it <u>on the Internet</u>.

3. **Q:** If Minh didn't like his meal in a restaurant, _____ ?
   A: He would complain <u>to the restaurant manager</u>.

4. **Q:** If he wrote a letter of complaint, _____ ?
   A: He would include <u>an explanation of the problem</u>.

5. **Q:** If you wrote a business letter, _____ ?
   A: I would put my return address <u>at the top</u>.

6. **Q:** If you sent the letter, _____ ?
   A: I would expect an answer <u>in about two weeks</u>.

7. **Q:** If they had a problem, _____ ?
   A: They would complain <u>because they would expect better service next time</u>.

G. **Write three contrary-to-fact conditional questions that you could ask your partner about his or her financial situation.**

1. What would you do if you lost your job? _____

2. _____

3. _____

4. _____

H. **Write what you think your partner would say.**

1. If Leah lost her job, she would go back to school. _____

2. _____

3. _____

4. _____

PRACTICE TEST

A. Look at the Jacobs' monthly budget and choose the best answer.

Monthly Expenses for June	Budgeted Amount	Actual Amount Spent
Auto (loan, gas, repairs)	$1,400	$1,560
Phone (home and mobile)	$130	$127.43
Satellite TV	$120	$120
Internet	$39.95	$39.95
Entertainment	$200	$140
Groceries	$780	$775
Medical	$300	$0
Mortgage	$2,200	$2,200
Retirement	$0	$0
Utilities (gas, electricity, water)	$270	$265
TOTAL		

1. How much did the Jacobs spend this month?

   a. $5,439.95

   b. $5,227.38

   c. $5,439

   d. $5,227

2. What did they not budget enough money for?

   a. auto

   b. groceries

   c. mortgage

   d. utilities

3. What's one area they aren't spending any money, but should be?

   a. gas for their cars

   b. cell phone

   c. retirement

   d. electricity

4. What did they budget for but not spend any money on this month?

   a. retirement

   b. medical expenses

   c. clothing

   d. gym membership

L E S S O N **1** The American dream

GOAL ■ Interpret housing advertisements

A. A noun is a person, place, or thing. Adjectives are words that describe nouns. Categorize each word below according to its part of speech.

barbecue	cozy	huge	kid-friendly
patio	pool	quiet	suburban
yard	miles	nice	freeways

<u>**NOUNS**</u>   <u>**ADJECTIVES**</u>

_____   _____

_____   _____

_____   _____

_____   _____

_____   _____

_____   _____

B. Read the housing ads. Circle the correct answer in the questions below.

#1 Make an Offer

Cozy, three-bedroom, 3.5-bath home located in a quiet suburban neighborhood about 10 miles from the city. Nice yard with a patio and barbecue. Come see and make an offer! **$475,000**

#2 Family Friendly

Single-family, 5-bedroom, 4-bath home for sale in a great kid-friendly neighborhood. Close to shopping, freeways, and public transportation. Huge backyard with pool and barbecue pit. **$750,000**

1. Which house is bigger?   House #1   (House #2)
2. Which house is the least expensive?   House #1   House #2
3. Which house is the smallest?   House #1   House #2
4. Which backyard is larger?   House #1   House #2

C. Study the chart.

Comparative and Superlative Adjectives			
Type of adjective	Simple form	Comparative form	Superlative form
One-syllable adjectives	cheap	cheaper	the cheapest
One-syllable adjectives that end in -*e*	safe	safer	the safest
One-syllable adjectives that end in *consonant-vowel-consonant*	big	bigger	the biggest
Two-syllable adjectives that end in -*y*	cozy	cozier	the coziest
Other two-syllable adjectives	recent	more recent	the most recent
Some two-syllable adjectives have two forms.	quiet	quieter or more quiet	the quietest or the most quiet
	friendly	friendlier or more friendly	the friendliest or the most friendly
Adjectives with three or more syllables	expensive	more expensive	the most expensive

- Use the comparative form to compare two things.
- If the second item is expressed, use ***than***.
    *New York is **bigger than** Los Angeles.*
- Use the superlative form to compare one thing to two or more things.
- A prepositional phrase is sometimes used at the end of a superlative sentence.
    *My town is the friendliest town **in the world**.*

D. Check (✓) the correct comparative or superlative form.

1. Her neighborhood is _____ than ours. ☐ the least expensive ☐ less expensive

2. They bought _____ house in the neighborhood. ☐ the prettiest ☐ a more pretty

3. You want to buy _____ house in the area. ☐ the secluded ☐ the most secluded

4. Our old house had _____ yard than this one. ☐ the biggest ☐ a bigger

5. Luis is buying the apartment on _____ floor. ☐ the most high ☐ the highest

6. Which city is _____ in the state? ☐ the safest ☐ the more safer

7. The people in our building are _____ than the people in hers. ☐ friendlier ☐ the friendliest

8. I want to buy _____ house I can afford. ☐ the most expensive ☐ the more expensive

E. Write comparative sentences. Use *than* when comparing two things.

1. Oakville is / friendly / my old town   *Oakville is friendlier than my old town.*

2. the house is / expensive / the condominium   _____

3. the bedroom is / dark / kitchen   _____

4. I want a / comfortable / living room   _____

5. the other house has / pretty / gardens   _____

6. I want a house / close / to the schools   _____

7. this old house is / cheap / that new house   _____

8. the new house has / a / big / backyard   _____

9. your agent charges / low fees / my agent   _____

F. Write superlative sentences using the words in parentheses.

1. He bought a house. (cheap / in Baytown)

   He bought the cheapest house in Baytown.

2. I have an apartment. (spacious / in my building)

   _____

3. Before buying a house, you should look at sales. (recent / in the neighborhood)

   _____

4. She is using the real estate agency that charges a fee. (low / of all the agencies)

   _____

5. I plan to negotiate with the seller. (motivated / of all the homeowners)

   _____

6. We live in a cottage. (cozy / on the street)

   _____

G. Write sentences comparing the place you live with the place where a family member or friend lives. Use comparative and superlative adjectives.

1. *Taj's apartment is larger than mine.* _____

2. _____

3. _____

LESSON ② Bigger? Better?

GOAL ■ Compare types of housing

A. Brainstorm adjectives that are positive and negative in regards to housing. Some can be both. Put them in the correct circle.

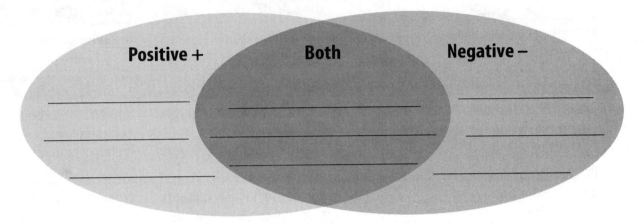

Positive +

Both

Negative −

_____   _____   _____

_____   _____   _____

_____   _____   _____

B. Look at the chart comparing the two homes. Answer the questions below.

House	Advantages	Disadvantages
	bigger closer to the city 2-car garage	noisy neighborhood more expensive to keep up
Condo		
	quiet street no yard to maintain	smaller association dues noisy neighbors no parking

1. Which one is bigger, the condo or the house? _____ *the house* _____

2. Which place is in a quieter neighborhood? _____

3. Which one has better parking? _____

4. Which place is closer to the city? _____

C. Study the chart.

Comparative and Superlative Questions				
Question word	**Subject**	**Verb**	**Adjective (+ noun)**	**Rule**
Which	one area	**is**	**bigger?** **the safest?**	Use **be** when following with an adjective.
Which	one area	**has**	**more rooms?** **the biggest floor plan?**	Use **have** before an adjective + noun.
Question		**Short answer**	**Long answer**	**Rule**
Which one **is bigger,** the condominium or the house?		The condominium.	The condominium **is bigger than** the house. The condominium **is bigger.**	When talking about two things and mentioning both of them, use **than**.
Which place **has more rooms,** the condominium or the house?		The house.	The house **has more rooms than** the condominium. The house **has more rooms.**	When talking about two things but only mentioning one of them, do not use **than**.

D. Complete each question with *is* or *has*.

1. Which house ____has____ a bigger master suite?

2. Which place _____ the least expensive?

3. Which house _____ the biggest backyard?

4. Which seller _____ the most motivated?

5. Which home _____ the most recent upgrades?

6. Which condominium _____ older?

7. Which property _____ the newest kitchen?

8. Which bank _____ the best interest rate?

9. Which cottage _____ the most secluded?

10. Which one _____ more patio space, the apartment or the condo?

11. Which home _____ closer to the freeway?

E. Write a complete answer for each question. Begin each sentence with the underlined words and use *than* in the answer.

1. Which house is cheaper, <u>the old one</u> or the new one?

   <u>The old one is cheaper than the new one.</u>

2. Which neighborhood is safer, the Oak Street neighborhood or <u>the State Road neighborhood</u>?

   _____

3. Which real estate agency has more agents, Real Homes or <u>True Life</u>?

   _____

4. Which home inspector is more careful, <u>Mrs. Poulin</u> or Mr. Reilly?

   _____

5. Which bank has lower interest rates, <u>Newtown Bank</u> or National Bank?

   _____

6. Which property has more amenities, the condominium or <u>the country cottage</u>?

   _____

7. Which home is closer to your job, the condo in the gated community or the condo in the high rise?

   _____

F. Look at the ads in Exercise B on page 44. Write three questions using comparative and superlative adjectives.

1. <u>Which home has more bedrooms?</u>

2. _____

3. _____

4. _____

G. Write answers to the questions you wrote in Exercise F.

1. <u>The second home has more bedrooms than the first home.</u>

2. _____

3. _____

4. _____

LESSON ③ Housing preferences

GOAL ■ Identify housing preferences

A. **Describe the following terms in your own words.**

1. fixer-upper: _____

2. newly remodeled: _____

3. brand-new build: _____

4. tear down: _____

B. **Which type of house would you rather buy? Why?**

_____

_____

C. **Interview two classmates and write their answers in the columns below.**

Questions	Classmate #1	Classmate #2
1. Does your house have three bedrooms?		
2. Does your house have a yard?		
3. Is your home in a quiet neighborhood?		
4. How many bathrooms does your home have?		
5. How many parking spaces do you have?		
6. Where is your home located?		

D. **Write three comparative or superlative statements about the information in Exercise C.**

1. Eric's home has more bedrooms than Monica's. _____

2. _____

3. _____

4. _____

E. Study the chart.

Yes/No and Information Questions	
Yes/No question	Short answer
Do you want air-conditioning?	Yes, I do. / No, I don't.
Do they need a garage?	Yes, they do. / No, they don't.
Does the house have a pool?	Yes, it does. / No, it doesn't.
Wh- question	Answer
What type of property do you want?	I want a house.
How many bedrooms does it have?	It has three bedrooms.
Where is it?	It's on High Street.
How much can you put down?	I can put down $10,000.
• *Wh-* questions start with *who, what, where, when, why*, or *how*.	

F. Read each statement. First, write a *Yes/No* question with the words in parentheses in your notebook. Then, write a short answer.

1. I want a pool. (you)   Do you want a pool?   (no)   No, I don't.

2. You prefer a two-car garage. (Tan)   _____   (yes)   _____

3. They want a fixer-upper. (we)   _____   (no)   _____

4. Ana needs an enclosed yard. (you)   _____   (yes)   _____

5. I like the new patio. (Maria)   _____   (no)   _____

6. We have to make an offer. (you)   _____   (yes)   _____

G. Unscramble the words to write *Wh-* questions.

1. price range / what / your / is   What is your price range?

2. you / how / want / bathrooms / do / many   _____

3. your / is / who / real estate agent   _____

4. time / is / this Sunday / what / the open house   _____

5. the counteroffer / is / much / how   _____

6. when / do / the inspection / the inspector / can   _____

H. Imagine you are a realtor asking your client what he is looking for in a home. Write questions using the information given.

1. (bathrooms) _How many bathrooms do you need?_____

2. (price range) _____

3. (bedrooms) _____

4. (air-conditioning) _____

5. (yard) _____

6. (housing type) _____

7. (neighborhood) _____

I. Write answers to the questions above for your imaginary client.

1. _____

2. _____

3. _____

4. _____

5. _____

6. _____

7. _____

J. Based on those answers, write an ad for the perfect place for your client.

_____

_____

_____

_____

_____

LESSON ④ Step-by-step

GOAL ■ Identify the steps to buying a home

A. Read the conversation below. Try to fill in the blanks with an appropriate word.

Jenna: My house is good. Her house is better. But his house is _____the best_____.

Aaron: Really? But his house is so far away.

Michelle: Yes, my house is farther. But her house is _____.

Jenna: Yeah, and she paid a lot of money for that house. I paid more for mine. But they paid

_____ for theirs.

Aaron: And they have a bad mortgage. Although mine is worse and Jenna's is

_____.

Michelle: True. You all do have bad mortgages. You bought when interest rates were high.

B. What are the four words in the underlined spaces in Exercise A? What do they have in common?

the best _____

_____

_____

_____

C. Match the words from Exercise B with the following comparative adjectives.

1. more   a. the farthest
2. farther   b. the worst
3. better   c. the most
4. worse   d. the best

D. Study the list of comparative and superlative adjectives and adverbs.

Irregular Comparative and Superlative Adjectives and Adverbs			
	Simple form	**Comparative form**	**Superlative form**
Irregular adjectives	good bad far little much/many	better worse farther less more	the best the worst the farthest the least the most
Irregular adverbs	well badly a little a lot	better worse less more	the best the worst the least the most

E. Using words from the chart above, complete the following sentences.

1. My house is _____ , but my friend's house is _____ .

2. My lunch was _____ today, but yesterday it was _____ .

3. I slept _____ last night, but night before last I slept _____ .

4. I was feeling _____ yesterday, but today I feel _____ .

F. Circle the correct sentence.

1. Think best before buying your next house. / (Think well before buying your next house.)

2. Look for the best real estate agent in the business. / Look for the bester real estate agent in the business.

3. Ask most questions if necessary. / Ask more questions if necessary.

4. Take the most time comparing prices. / Take the more time comparing prices.

5. Don't spend more than you can afford. / Don't spend morer than you can afford.

6. Choose the home that you like the bestest. / Choose the home that you like the best.

7. Find the home that needs the less amount of work. / Find the home that needs the least amount of work.

8. Choose the house with the better price. / Choose the house with the more better price.

9. Don't buy the home that is farthest from your job. / Don't buy the home that is farther from your job.

G. **Complete each sentence with the comparative or superlative form of the word in parentheses.**

1. (good) I think May is _____the best_____ month to buy a house.

2. (many) There are _____ houses available in the spring than in the winter.

3. (good) Homebuyers sometimes get _____ prices in the spring than in the winter.

4. (little) Unfortunately, good real estate agents are _____ available in the spring than in the winter.

5. (bad) Sometimes banks have _____ mortgage terms in the spring.

6. (well) Some people don't use an agent, but you can negotiate _____ if you have one.

7. (a lot) If you can't find the right house, you may have to tell your agent to look around

   _____ .

8. (little) Don't buy a home in _____ desirable neighborhood.

9. (more) Find a home with _____ space for the money.

H. **Look back at the conversation in Exercise A. Write similar sentences using the words in parentheses and comparing places where people live.**

1. (a little) My aunt paid a little in taxes this year. My cousin paid less. I paid the least.

2. (bad) _____

   _____

3. (well) _____

   _____

4. (many) _____

   _____

5. (a little) _____

   _____

LESSON **5** Financial planning

GOAL ■ Interpret mortgage information

A. Complete each sentence with the correct word or phrase.

afford	credit check	down payment
mortgage	price range	purchase price

1. If you can't _____ to buy a house with cash, you will need to get a

   _____ .

2. Make sure you look for a house that is in your _____ , one that you can afford the monthly mortgage payments for.

3. Before you get a mortgage, they will need to run a _____ .

4. You should try to save up enough money for a 10-20% _____ .

5. You will work with the realtor who will negotiate the _____ with the seller.

B. Imagine you are thinking about buying a new house. What should you do? Make a list with a group.

Home-Buying Checklist

✓ Find a realtor

✓

✓

✓

✓

✓

C. Study the chart.

Should and Should Have	
Should	*Should have*
You **should analyze** your financial situation before getting a mortgage.	You **should have analyzed** your financial situation before getting a mortgage.
She **shouldn't buy** a house in that neighborhood.	She **shouldn't have bought** a house in that neighborhood.
Should we **use** a realtor?	**Should** we **have used** a realtor?
Where **should** we **keep** our financial documents?	Where **should** we **have kept** our financial documents?
• To give or ask for advice about a present situation, use *should* + base verb. • To express regret about a past situation, use *should have* + past participle.	

D. Use the answer in parentheses to tell the people what they should or should not do.

1. Should I use a realtor?   (yes)   <u>Yes, you should use a realtor.</u>

2. Should he get approved for a loan first?   (yes)   _____

3. Should she think about her price range?   (yes)   _____

4. Should I buy something that I can't afford?   (no)   _____

5. Shouldn't we negotiate the purchase price?   (yes)   _____

6. Should they get a balloon mortgage?   (no)   _____

7. Shouldn't she buy her own place?   (no)   _____

8. Should we save money for a deposit?   (yes)   _____

9. Should we put down 0%?   (no)   _____

E. Take the positive statements from above and rewrite them using *should have*.

1. <u>You should have used a realtor.</u>

2. _____

3. _____

4. _____

5. _____

F. Use the words in parentheses to tell the people what they should or should not have done.

1. I didn't compare prices. (compare prices)

   You should have compared prices.

2. He didn't meet with a financial planner. (meet with a financial planner)

   _____

3. We bought the first house we saw. (look around)

   _____

4. She found a realtor online. (ask for a recommendation)

   _____

5. They used a discount broker. (not trust his advice)

   _____

6. He signed up for an adjustable rate mortgage (ARM). (get a fixed rate loan)

   _____

7. They sold their house after the market dropped. (wait for market recovery)

   _____

G. Look back at your checklist in Exercise B. Take the first three things you wrote and write *should* statements.

1. *I should find a realtor.* _____

2. _____

3. _____

4. _____

H. Look back at your checklist in Exercise B. Take the last three things you wrote and write *should have* statements.

1. *I should have found a realtor.* _____

2. _____

3. _____

4. _____

PRACTICE TEST

A. Read the housing advertisements and choose the best answer.

#1 Make it Your Own

Quaint, two-bedroom,1.5-bath home located outside the city. Great fixer-upper with lots of potential. Big yard with a built-in jacuzzi. Come see it and make an offer!
$350,000

#2 Family Friendly

Single-family, 3-bedroom, 4-bath home for sale in a great neighborhood near the park. Huge backyard with pool, jacuzzi, and barbecue pit.
$750,000

1. How much will it cost you to buy the house that needs some work done?
   a. $350,000
   b. $550,000
   c. $650,000
   d. $750,000

2. Which house is close to the freeways and would be good for someone who has to commute?
   a. house #1
   b. house #2
   c. both house #1 and #2
   d. The ads don't say.

3. Which house has a jacuzzi in the backyard?
   a. house #1
   b. house #2
   c. both house #1 and #2
   d. neither house #1 or house #2

4. Which house would be better for a family with small children?
   a. house #1
   b. house #2
   c. both house #1 and #2
   d. neither house #1 or house #2

5. Which house is in the downtown area of the city?
   a. house #1
   b. house #2
   c. both house #1 and #2
   d. neither house #1 or house #2

LESSON **1** Your community

GOAL ■ Locate community resources

A. Write the places where you can do these things in your community.

Task	Places I can go	Task	Places I can go
borrow a book		mail a package	
go swimming		send daughter to preschool	
get stamps		recycle	
volunteer		register a car	

B. Write questions and answers about the tasks and places in the chart in Exercise A.

1. *Where do you borrow a book?* _____   _____
2. _____   _____
3. _____   _____
4. _____   _____
5. _____   _____
6. _____   _____
7. _____   _____
8. _____   _____

C. If you wanted to find the addresses of the places above, what would you do? Check (✓) the appropriate column.

Places	Call	Go online	Ask a friend
Post Office			
DMV			
Bank			
School			
Park			

D. Study the chart.

Embedded Questions: *Wh-* Questions		
Wh- question	Introductory question	Embedded question
Where is Orange Avenue?	Can you show me	**where** Orange Avenue **is?**
When does the library **open?**	Do you know	**when** the library **opens?**
Who is the manager?	Could you tell me	**who** the manager **is?**
What is the address?	Would you tell me	**what** the address **is?**

- An embedded question is a question that is placed within another question or statement.
- Use an embedded question to make a question more polite.
- In an embedded *Wh-* question, the subject comes before the verb.
- The auxiliaries *do/does* are not used in embedded questions.

E. Find the introductory question. Underline it. Find the *Wh-* question in each embedded question. Write the *Wh-* questions on the lines.

1. <u>Will you show me</u> where the stores are? Where are the stores?

2. Can you tell me when the bus comes? _____

3. Would you show me where the station is? _____

4. Do you know who the museum director is? _____

5. Do you remember what his name is? _____

6. Can you explain why you were late? _____

7. Do you know how I can join the book club? _____

8. Will you explain what the rules are? _____

9. Could you tell me when the bank closes? _____

10. Can you show me where Olive Ave. is? _____

11. Do you know when the store opens? _____

F. **Change each question to an embedded question using the expression in parentheses.**

1. When does the Department of Motor Vehicles open? (Do you know . . .)

   Do you know when the Department of Motor Vehicles opens?

2. Where is the skate park? (Can you explain . . .)

   _____

3. What time does the senior center close? (Do you remember . . .)

   _____

4. Why isn't the health clinic open today? (Can you tell me . . .)

   _____

5. What days is the library open? (Do you know . . .)

   _____

6. Who is head of the Chamber of Commerce? (Could you tell me . . .)

   _____

7. What time do the buses stop running at night? (Would you tell me . . .)

   _____

G. **Imagine you are new to the community. Think of five things you might want to know. Write embedded questions you might ask someone from the community.**

1. *Do you know where I can use a computer?*

2. _____

3. _____

4. _____

5. _____

6. _____

LESSON **2** Can you tell me . . . ?

GOAL ■ Use the telephone

A. **Where would you go to do each of the following things? Write one idea on each line.**

1. Go bowling   _Great Lanes Bowling_ _____

2. See a movie   _____

3. Find an exercise class   _____

4. Donate books   _____

5. Recycle paper and bottles   _____

6. Get a marriage license   _____

7. Register for computer classes   _____

B. **Use the places you listed in Exercise A and ask questions about your community. Follow the example.**

1. _Do you know if there is a bowling alley around here?_ _____

2. _____

3. _____

4. _____

5. _____

6. _____

7. _____

C. **If you wanted more information about the places below, such as hours or services offered, would you call, go online, or stop by? Check (✓) the appropriate column.**

Places	Call	Go online	Stop by
Movie theatre			
Library			
City Hall			
School			
Gym			

D. Study the chart.

Embedded Questions: *Yes/No* Questions		
Yes/No question	**Introductory question**	**Embedded question**
Is the library near here?	Can you tell me	**if** the library **is** near here?
Does the pool **open** at 8:00?	Do you know	**if** the pool **opens** at 8:00?
Does the museum **close** at 9:00?	Do you remember	**if** the museum **closes** at 9:00?

- For *Yes/No* questions, use *if* before the embedded question.
- In embedded *Yes/No* questions, the subject usually comes before the verb. One exception is embedded *Yes/No* questions with *there is/there are*.
  Can you tell me if **there is** a bank in this neighborhood?
- The auxiliaries *do/does* are not used in embedded questions.

E. Find the *Yes/No* question in each embedded question. Write the *Yes/No* question on the lines.

1. Do you know if the store opens at 10 a.m.?

   Does the store open at 10 a.m.?
   _____

2. Can you tell me if the high school is near here?

   _____

   _____

3. Do you remember if the bookstore closes at 9 p.m.?

   _____

   _____

4. Would you tell me if the French restaurant takes reservations?

   _____

   _____

5. Could you tell me if the health clinic is open on Sundays?

   _____

   _____

6. Can you tell me if the bank closes before 5 p.m.?

   _____

   _____

7. Do you know if the post office is near here?

   _____

   _____

8. Can you remember if the pool is indoors?

   _____

   _____

9. Do you know if they do street sweeping on Tuesdays?

   _____

   _____

F. **Change each question to an embedded question using the expression in parentheses.**

1. Is the library open today? (Do you know . . .)
   Do you know if the library is open today?

2. Does the library have an extensive collection of audiovisual materials? (Do you know . . .)

3. Can the reference materials be checked out? (Do you remember . . .)

4. Am I allowed to check out two videos at a time? (Can you tell me . . .)

5. Is the reading room open every Tuesday? (Do you know . . .)

6. Can I access the Internet at the library? (Could you tell me . . .)

7. Is there a time limit for using the computers? (Can you tell me . . .)

8. Are there computers in the children's reading room? (Do you know . . .)

9. Does the library offer a literacy program? (Would you tell me . . .)

10. Does the library need volunteers to help out? (Do you know . . .)

11. Is there a room available for public meetings? (Do you remember . . .)

G. **Write embedded questions using the information given.**

1. (do you know, pool, Tuesday)
   Do you know if the pool is open on Tuesday?

2. (can you tell me, skate park, age requirement)

3. (do you remember, adult school, Orange Ave.)

4. (do you know, bookstore, used books)

LESSON ③ Why don't we . . . ?

GOAL ■ Give suggestions

A. Read the conversation.

Marna: What should we do tomorrow night?

Claudia: <u>How about seeing a movie?</u>

Marna: That sounds great. Let's go to dinner first at that new Japanese restaurant. I've been craving sushi!

Claudia: Sounds good to me. We could get some chocolate for dessert at the candy shop next door.

Marna: Why don't we walk? All this talk of food and chocolate is making me fat!

B. There are four suggestions in the conversation above. Underline them and write the suggestions on the lines.

1. _How about seeing a movie?_____

2. _____

3. _____

4. _____

C. Write the part of the suggestion that comes before the verb in Exercise B.

1. _How about_____

2. _____

3. _____

4. _____

D. Study the chart on making suggestions.

Making Suggestions		
Suggestion phrase	**Base verb**	**Suggestion**
Why don't we	go	to the park?
Do you want to	see	a movie?
Let's	invite	him.
We could	eat	at the café.
Suggestion phrase	**Verb + *-ing***	**Suggestion**
How about	joining	a book club?

E. Find the mistake in each sentence and rewrite the sentence correctly.

1. We could seeing a movie tonight.

   We could see a movie tonight.

2. Why we don't go to the bookstore?

   _____

3. Let's taking Mom to a nice restaurant for her birthday.

   _____

4. Do you want play baseball in the park?

   _____

5. How about go to a museum this afternoon?

   _____

6. Let join the community center.

   _____

7. We could walked to the movie.

   _____

8. Do you want see a movie?

   _____

9. How about we eat at the Corner Grill?

   _____

F. Unscramble the words to write suggestions.

1. train / could / to run / in the marathon / we / .

   We could train to run in the marathon.

2. we / use / the computers / don't / at the library / why / ?

   _____

3. taking / how / guitar lessons / about / ?

   _____

4. want / do / volunteer / to / you / at the hospital / ?

   _____

5. eat / at the new Italian restaurant / let's / tonight / .

   _____

6. could / we / in the public pool / swim / .

   _____

7. looking / about / for an apartment / on the community bulletin board / how / ?

   _____

G. Imagine that you and a friend are going out for the evening. Write a conversation that includes at least four suggestions.

You: _____

Your partner: _____

You: _____

Your partner: _____

You: _____

Your partner: _____

You: _____

Your partner: _____

You: _____

Your partner: _____

LESSON **4** How far is it?

GOAL ■ Interpret a road map

A. Read the following statements and draw a map on a separate piece of paper.

1. There is a campground in the north.
2. Interstate 5 runs north-south.
3. There is a hotel in the southwest corner.
4. Exit 48 off of Interstate 5 is in the middle.
5. There is a hospital in the south and another one in the northwest corner.
6. There is a rest area at Exit 47, which is south of Exit 48.
7. State scenic Highway 91 runs east-west.
8. There is a lake at the eastern end of Highway 91.

B. Turn the following statements into questions about your community.

1. You are curious about how far it is to the next city.

   <u>How far is it to the next city?</u>

2. You want to know how far it is to the next state.

   _____

3. You are wondering which highway is the most crowded during rush hour.

   _____

4. You would like to know if there is a hospital in your city.

   _____

5. Your friend wants to know how far it is to the nearest mountains.

   _____

6. You have no idea if there is a lake close enough for boating.

   _____

C. Study the chart.

Indirect Questions		
	Direct question	**Indirect question**
Wh- Question	He asked, "**Where is** the campground?" They asked, "**How far are** you **going**?"	He asked **where** the campground **was**. They asked **how far** you **were going**.
Yes/No Question	You asked, "**Are** we **stopping** now?" We asked, "**Did** you **see** the rest stop?"	You asked **if** we **were stopping** now. We asked **if** you **had seen** the rest stop.

- An indirect question reports on what someone asked.
- Use statement word order in an indirect question. Use a period at the end.
- For *Yes/No* questions, use *if* before the subject.
- Follow this sequence of tenses:

Direct Question	Indirect Question
simple present	simple past
present continuous	past continuous
simple past	past perfect

D. Find the mistake in each reported question. Rewrite the question correctly.

1. I asked where the parks are located.

   I asked where the parks were located.
   _____

2. She asked if he coming.

   _____

3. You asked if we turned left at the corner.

   _____

4. He ask which highway we were taking.

   _____

5. They asked if we stopped now.

   _____

6. I asked how far you went.

   _____

7. We asked if we missed the turnoff.

   _____

E. Change each direct question to an indirect question. Use *if* for *Yes/No* questions.

1. He asked, "How does she get to the mountains?"

    He asked how she got to the mountains.

2. My mother wondered, "Do they go to the beach every year?"

    _____

3. The man asked, "When is the highway going to be closed for road work?"

    _____

4. Her parents asked, "What time does the train leave?"

    _____

5. Marna questioned, "Is there a faster way to get to the outlet mall?"

    _____

6. Felipe asked, "Did you rent a car for that road trip?"

    _____

7. They asked, "When is she driving to the East Coast?"

    _____

8. I wondered, "Is the scenic highway faster than the interstate?"

    _____

9. Jenny asked, "What time does the rest stop close?"

    _____

F. Choose four questions from Exercise B and write indirect questions.

1. I asked how far it was to the next city. _____

2. _____

3. _____

4. _____

5. _____

LESSON **5** Volunteering

GOAL ■ Identify ways to volunteer in the community

A. Imagine that you are thinking about volunteering somewhere in your community. Make a list of things you could do. (For example: walk dogs, work with children)

	Things I Can Do
✓	Join a Neighborhood Watch group
✓	
✓	
✓	
✓	

B. Write places where you might volunteer. Ask your partner to suggest some places you might volunteer. Write your partner's suggestions below.

	Places to Volunteer
✓	Senior citizens' center
✓	
✓	
✓	
✓	

C. Study the chart.

Can, Could, and Should	
Example	**Rule**
You **can** eat at the Mexican restaurant. We **could** go to the bookstore.	*Can* and *could* are used to offer a suggestion when there is more than one choice.
They **should** go to the library today. You **shouldn't** be late for your class.	*Should/shouldn't* is used when there is a recommended choice.
• *Can* and *could* have the same meaning when making suggestions. • *Could* does not have a past meaning in this case.	

D. Complete each sentence with *can*, *could*, or *should*. In some cases, more than one answer is possible.

1. My daughter has to get volunteer hours in order to graduate so she _____should_____ call the school to see where she can volunteer.

2. If you want to be a volunteer, you _____ ask if they need someone at the senior center.

3. You _____ also try the library, the community center, or the hospital.

4. If you like to work with animals, you _____ call the animal shelter to see if they are looking for volunteers.

5. My friend likes to work with numbers. I keep telling him he _____ volunteer to be the treasurer for a nonprofit organization.

6. I like to read to children so I _____ volunteer at a library or an elementary school.

7. My sister likes to take care of sick people so she _____ volunteer at a nursing home or a health clinic.

8. Her brother likes books. He _____ see if they need any volunteers at the school library.

9. Brian doesn't like kids very much so he _____ volunteer at the daycare center.

10. But he does like elderly people so maybe he _____ help out at the senior center.

E. Read each statement and write *should* statements about what each person should do as a volunteer.

1. Emily loves animals.

   She should work at an animal shelter.

2. Erin and Eli like to teach people to read.

   _____

3. He likes to keep track of money.

   _____

4. She likes to spend time with children.

   _____

5. James likes to organize things.

   _____

F. Read each statement and write *could* statements about what each person could do as a volunteer. Try to suggest two places for each person to work.

1. Lyle enjoys working with animals.

   He could volunteer at an animal shelter or kennel.

2. Kirsten likes to cook and clean.

   _____

3. Enrique likes to make phone calls.

   _____

4. Bita enjoys making decorations.

   _____

5. Ariana likes working with kids.

   _____

G. Write a short paragraph about what you like to do and some places you could volunteer. Use *can*, *could*, and *should*.

_____

_____

_____

_____

_____

PRACTICE TEST

A. Read the map and choose the best answer.

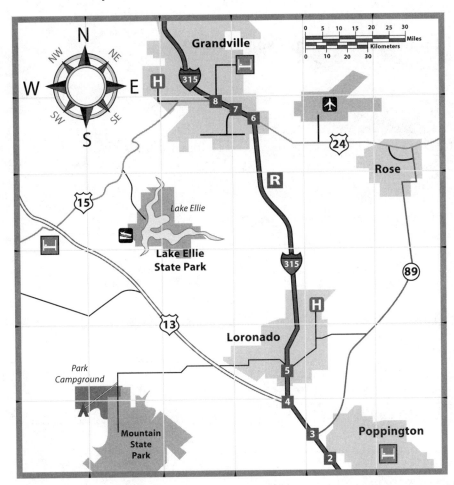

1. What city in located in the north?

   a. Grandville

   b. Rose

   c. Loronado

   d. Poppington

2. What is located in the middle of the 315, the 15, and the 13?

   a. the airport

   b. Lake Ellie State Park

   c. Mountain State Park

   d. the park campground

3. The airport is located between _____.

   a. Lake Ellie State Park and the hotel

   b. Grandville and Loronado

   c. the 315 and the 24

   d. Grandville and Rose

4. What city is located where the 13 and 315 cross?

   a. Grandville

   b. Rose

   c. Loronado

   d. Poppington

LESSON ❶ Health habits

GOAL ■ Identify health habits

A. Make a list of your healthy and unhealthy habits.

Healthy Habits	Unhealthy Habits
walking	eating junk food

B. How long have you done each of these habits? Write your answers.

1. I have eaten junk food since I was a child. _____

2. _____

3. _____

4. _____

C. Answer the following questions about yourself.

1. Have you ever read a nutrition label? _____

2. Have you ever run a race? _____

3. Have you ever played a sport? If so, which one? _____

4. Have you ever smoked? _____

D. Write statements about yourself answering each of the questions above.

1. Yes, I have read a nutrition label. or No, I have never read a nutrition label. _____

2. _____

3. _____

4. _____

E. **Study the chart.**

Present Perfect				
Affirmative statement	**Subject**	*Has/Have*	**Past participle**	
	He	has	eaten	five pieces of fruit today.
Negative statement	**Subject**	*Has/Have*	*not/never*	**Past participle**
	You	have	never	**been** to a doctor.
Yes/No question	*Has/Have*	**Subject**	**Past participle**	
	Have	**you**	**walked**	a lot this week?
Wh- **question**	*Wh-* **word**	*Has/Have*	**Subject**	**Past participle**
	How long	has	he	**had** a cold?

- Use the present perfect to show: (a) something happened at an unspecified time in the past; (b) something happened more than once in the past; (c) something started at a specific time in the past and continues in the present.

F. **Complete each sentence with the correct present perfect form of the verb in parentheses.**

1. (take) He _____has taken_____ illegal drugs before.

2. (exercise) She _____ every day since she started her diet.

3. (drink) He _____ coffee ever since he went away to college.

4. (not, move) Elia _____ off the couch since she hurt her back.

5. (run) _____ they ever _____ a marathon?

6. (not, eat) He _____ any protein today.

7. (take) We _____ never _____ vitamins before.

8. (not, eat) I _____ at that fast-food restaurant since I got sick last year.

9. (sleep) Rob _____ eight hours every night for the past month.

10. (see) _____ you ever _____ a doctor about your cough?

11. (not, play) We _____ sports since we were kids.

G. Write present perfect questions and complete answers using the words provided.

1. **Q:** (she / swim / every day this week) <u>Has she swum every day this week?</u>

   A: (yes) <u>Yes, she has swum every day this week.</u>

2. **Q:** (how long / she / be / a swimmer) _____

   A: (for three years) _____

3. **Q:** (how many times / she / swim / this week) _____

   A: (five times) _____

4. **Q:** (she / ever / got / injured from swimming) _____

   A: (no / never) _____

5. **Q:** (she / ever / compete / in any swimming events) _____

   A: (no / never) _____

6. **Q:** (why / not / she / tried) _____

   A: (because / she / not / want / to train) _____

7. **Q:** (she / this morning / has / vitamins / taken) _____

   A: (she / not / has / no) _____

H. Write sentences about your good and bad habits using the present perfect.

1. <u>I have walked every day since the doctor told me I needed to lose weight.</u>

2. _____

3. _____

4. _____

5. _____

LESSON **2** What's the problem?

GOAL ■ Describe symptoms of illnesses

A. Complete the following chart about yourself by putting checkmarks (✓) in the *yes* or *no* columns and writing answers in the *how long* column.

Habits	No	Yes	If yes, how long?
Exercising		✓	5 years
Drinking a lot of water every day			
Smoking			
Eating fruits and vegetables			
Going to the doctor			
Taking illegal drugs			
Sleeping at least eight hours at night			
Taking vitamins			
Stretching			
Walking every day			
Relaxing when stressed			
Going to the dentist			

B. How long have you done or not done each of these habits? Using the chart, write several statements about your habits.

I have never smoked. I have been exercising for five years.

_____

_____

_____

_____

_____

_____

C. Study the chart.

Present Perfect Continuous Statements					
	Subject	*Has/Have*	*Been*	Present participle	
Affirmative Statement	I	have	been	walking	30 minutes a day for the past month.
	I	have	been	exercising	for an hour.
	Subject	*Has/Have not*	*Been*	Present participle	
Negative Statement	He	hasn't	been	eating	healthy food lately.
	You	haven't	been	sleeping	enough recently.

- The present perfect continuous emphasizes the duration of an activity or state that started in the past and continues in the present. It also shows that an activity has been in progress recently.
- With some verbs (*work, live, teach*), there is no difference in meaning between the present perfect and the present perfect continuous: I **have lived/have been living** here since 2000.
- Some verbs are not usually used in the continuous form: *be, believe, hate, have, known, like, want.*

D. Circle the correct verb for each sentence.

1. Josef _____ to improve his health lately.   a. has trying   (b. has been trying)

2. He _____ a lot of fast food.   a. haven't been eating   b. hasn't been eating

3. You _____ well recently.   a. haven't been sleeping   b. haven't been sleep

4. You _____ about your schoolwork.   a. has been worrying   b. have been worrying

5. I _____ enough recently.   a. haven't been exercising   b. hasn't been exercising

6. And I _____ too many sweets.   a. have been eating   b. have been ate

7. We _____ good care of our teeth lately.   a. have been taken   b. have been taking

E. Complete each sentence with the present perfect continuous of the verb in parentheses.

1. (sit) I _____ have been sitting _____ on the couch all day.

2. (not / run) I _____ at all lately.

3. (eat) You _____ a lot of junk food recently.

4. (not / exercise) And you _____ at all.

5. (feel) Caterina _____ faint and dizzy today.

6. (not / follow) They _____ the doctor's instructions.

7. (not / take) They _____ their medicine.

F. **Circle the correct sentence.**

1. I have never been applying for health insurance. / (I have never applied for health insurance.)

2. He has had two heart attacks. / He has been having two heart attacks.

3. He has been knowing that doctor for five years. / He has known that doctor for five years.

4. I have been having two teeth pulled. / I have had two teeth pulled.

5. Have you ever had a blood test? / Have you ever been having a blood test?

6. We have never bought ibuprofen. / We have never been buying ibuprofen.

7. They have been sick all day. / They have been being sick all day.

8. She has been receiving treatment for two months. / She has been received treatment for two months.

9. You haven't ever been having a hernia. / You haven't ever had a hernia.

G. **Using the information given, write sentences that describe you. Use the present perfect or the present perfect continuous.**

1. (have, blood test) _I have never had a blood test._ _____

2. (have, health insurance) _____

3. (read, nutrition labels) _____

4. (see, doctor) _____

5. (look, pharmacy) _____

6. (pay, medical expenses) _____

7. (walk, school) _____

H. **Write present perfect continuous statements about your good and bad habits from Exercise A.**

1. (drinking a lot of water every day)

   I have been drinking a lot of water every day for five years. _____

2. (eat fruits and vegetables)

   _____

3. (go to the doctor)

   _____

4. (take vitamins)

   _____

5. (sleep at least eight hours a night)

   _____

GOAL ■ Interpret doctor's instructions

A. **Look at the list of doctors below and decide which doctor said each statement. Write the type of doctor on the line.**

| podiatrist | dentist | pediatrician | ophthalmologist | chiropractor | obstetrician |

1. "Your children need to eat healthier foods each day." _____

2. "Make sure you are taking your prenatal vitamins every day." _____

3. "You need to floss your teeth every time you brush them." _____

4. "You should buy some good walking shoes." _____

5. "Try to do these exercises three times a day to stretch your back." _____

6. "Always wear your glasses when typing on the computer." _____

B. **What is something else each of these doctors might say?**

1. dentist: _____

2. chiropractor: _____

3. podiatrist: _____

4. ophthalmologist: _____

5. pediatrician: _____

6. obstetrician: _____

C. **How would you tell someone what your doctor said? Imagine that you are telling your partner what four of these doctors said to you.**

1. My pediatrician said that my kids needed to eat healthier foods every day.

2. _____

3. _____

4. _____

5. _____

D. Study the chart.

Indirect Speech	
Direct speech	**Indirect speech**
"The most important thing **is** your health."	The doctor **said** (that) the most important thing **was** my health.
"You **eat** too much sugar."	The doctor **told me** (that) I **ate** too much sugar.

- Indirect speech reports on what someone has said.
- The use of *that* is optional in indirect speech.
- In indirect speech, you *say* something or you *tell* someone something.
- *Tell* is usually followed by an indirect object noun or pronoun.
- Other verbs like *say* are *agree, announce, answer, complain, explain, reply, state.*
- Other verbs like *tell* are *assure, advise, convince, notify, promise, remind, teach, warn.*
- Change the present tense in direct speech to the past tense in indirect speech.
- Change the pronouns to reflect the correct person.

E. Underline the indirect speech in each sentence.

1. I told you <u>I wanted to lose weight.</u>
2. My mother agreed that it was a good idea to add more fiber to my diet.
3. She said I needed to eat a balanced diet.
4. The doctor explained that dieting wasn't the only way to lose weight.
5. My friend told me she ran three miles a day to stay in shape.
6. Lola convinced me that exercise was an important part of staying healthy.
7. I said that I understood everything I have to do.
8. The physical therapist told me that I needed to stretch after exercising.
9. She told him she wanted to exercise more.
10. The dentist said that I needed to floss more often.
11. He complained that his back was hurting from too much sitting.

F. Change the direct speech to indirect speech.

1. My husband said, "There are five grams of protein in the soup."

   My husband said (that) there were five grams of protein in the soup.

2. Dr. Brown told me, "You need to check nutrition labels carefully."

   _____

3. He said, "It is important to check the number of calories and grams of fat per serving."

   _____

4. He also explained, "It is important to monitor sodium levels."

   _____

5. My mother always complained, "You eat too much saturated fat."

   _____

6. She warned me, "You have to pay attention to your cholesterol."

   _____

7. I said, "I know I need to stop eating junk food."

   _____

G. Complete the following quotes with what these people have said to you. Then, rewrite each quote using direct speech.

1. The nurse said, "It is a good idea to eat a larger lunch and smaller dinner."

   The nurse said it was a good idea to eat a larger lunch and a smaller dinner.

2. My mother always told me, "_____."

   _____

3. My father explained, "_____."

   _____

4. My friend warned me, "_____."

   _____

5. The doctor said to me, "_____."

   _____

LESSON **4** **Nutrition labels**

GOAL ■ Interpret nutrition information

A. **Check (✓) the items you think are important on a nutrition label. Then, decide which are the three most important.**

Nutrition label	Important	Nutrition label	Important
calories		sodium	
fat		vitamins	
cholesterol		protein	
fiber		carbohydrates	

What are the three most important?

_____ _____ _____

B. **Which label items would be of most importance based on the following relationships?**

1. Salt and high blood pressure   _sodium_ _____

2. Diets and weight loss   _____

3. Digestive health and the colon   _____

4. Arterial health and strokes   _____

5. Immune system and disease fighting   _____

C. **When you look at a nutrition label, what do you look for? Why?**

_____

_____

_____

_____

D. Study the chart.

Indirect Speech: Modals	
Direct speech	**Indirect speech**
He said, "I can read nutrition labels."	He said (that) he **could** read nutrition labels.
She said, "You may need some fiber." (may = possibility)	She said (that) she **might** need some fiber.
The doctor said, "You may start eating more fat." (may = permission)	The doctor said (that) I **could** start eating more fat.
I said, "I must stop eating so much sugar."	I said (that) I **had to** stop eating so much sugar.
They said, "We will start paying more attention to what we eat."	They said (that) they **would** start paying more attention to what they ate.
The modal **should** does not change form in indirect speech. He said, "You should eat more fruit." / He said (that) I should eat more fruit.	

E. Complete each sentence with the correct form of the modal in parentheses.

1. (will) I said that I _____would_____ drink plenty of fluids.

2. (may: possibility) He told her that she _____ need to start reading nutrition labels.

3. (should) Gina convinced me that I _____ start eating foods with more fiber.

4. (may: permission) His doctor told him that he _____ start eating foods with more fat.

5. (must) My sister said that she _____ start watching her weight.

6. (can) You said that I _____ buy junk food every once in a while.

7. (will) We warned you that you _____ get sick if you ate that.

8. (must) She said that he _____ start exercising.

9. (should) They convinced me that I _____ stop counting calories.

F. Change the direct speech to indirect speech.

1. "You must look for the saturated fat on nutrition labels."

   I told her that she had to look for the saturated fat on nutrition labels.

2. "You must start reading nutrition labels."

   My wife reminded me that _____.

3. "If he doesn't start counting calories, he may gain weight."

   They said that _____.

4. "We can start looking for foods that are high in protein."

   You explained that _____.

5. "I will add up the servings with my calculator."

   You told me _____.

6. "You should look for the amount of cholesterol in those chips."

   My friend suggested _____.

7. "Because of their high blood pressure, they may not eat foods that are high in fat."

   Their mother said _____.

G. Write statements about how you would like to change your health habits using modals.

1. (can) I could start eating more vegetables. _____

2. (may: possibility) _____

3. (should) _____

4. (must) _____

5. (can) _____

6. (will) _____

7. (may: permission) _____

H. Which habit do you think will be the hardest to change? Why?

_____

_____

_____

_____

LESSON **5** Do you want dental coverage?

GOAL ■ Complete a health insurance form

A. Do you have health insurance? If so, what does your plan cover? If you don't have health insurance, what would you like it to cover? Complete the checklist below.

Health Insurance Checklist	Yes	No
Low co-pay		
Dental coverage		
Vision coverage		
Discounted prescriptions		
My choice of doctors		
Low premiums		
Good reputation		
Gym membership		
Good customer service		
Easy to use website		

B. Circle the most important items in your health insurance in Exercise A.

C. What is most important to you and your family in health insurance? Why?

_____

_____

_____

_____

D. Study the chart.

	Has/Have	Subject	Been	Present participle
Present Perfect Continuous Questions				
	Has/Have	Subject	*Been*	Present participle
Yes/No Question	**Has** **Have** **Have**	he you they	**been**	**researching** insurance companies lately? **contacting** insurance agents? **filling out** their health history forms?
	Wh- word	*Has/Have*	Subject	*Been*	Present participle
Wh- Question	How long How long How long	**have** **has** **has**	they he she	**been**	**thinking** about insurance? **looking** for a new insurance company? **fighting** that claim?

E. Fix the mistake in each question below by writing the correct question on the line.

1. Has you been calling the insurance company?

   Have you been calling the insurance company?

2. What quotes have she been getting from the insurance companies?

   _____

3. Have they pay her insurance claim yet?

   _____

4. Has the insurance company sended them new cards yet?

   _____

5. What doctor has he be seeing?

   _____

6. Where has the insurance company been sent him?

   _____

7. Has the doctors been able to figure out what the problem is?

   _____

F. Write _Yes/No_ present perfect continuous questions and answers using the words given.

1. **Q:** she / see new eye doctor

   A: yes / two years

   Q: Has she been seeing a new eye doctor?

   A: Yes, she has been seeing a new eye doctor for two years.

2. **Q:** you / look for an insurance company

   A: no

   Q: _____

   A: _____

3. **Q:** we / look for a new doctor

   A: yes / since last month

   Q: _____

   A: _____

4. **Q:** he / fill out medical history form

   A: yes / for two hours

   Q: _____

   A: _____

5. **Q:** they / try to add vision to their plan

   A: no

   Q: _____

   A: _____

G. Unscramble the words to write _Wh-_ present perfect continuous questions.

1. taking / been / have / how long / allergy medicine / you

   How long have you been taking allergy medicine?

2. been / with warm salt water / how often / she / gargling / has

   _____

3. about their high blood pressure / who / consulting / they / have / been

   _____

4. what / in a health insurance plan / been / has / looking for / he

   _____

5. you / going / where / been / for your prenatal class / have

   _____

6. reading / haven't / been / the nutrition labels / you / why

   _____

A. Look at the bar graph and choose the best answer.

The Bad Health Habits of Ms. Tracy's Class

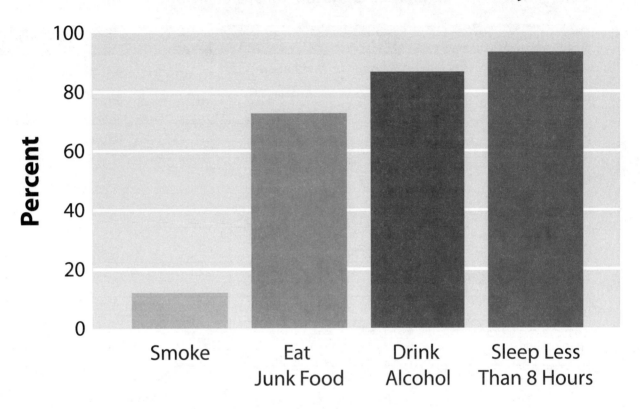

1. What percentage of people sleep less than 8 hours?
    a. 85%   b. 75%
    c. 95%   d. 100%

2. What bad habit do most of the students have?
    a. smoking   b. eating junk food
    c. drinking alcohol   d. sleeping less than 8 hours

3. What do 85% of the students do?
    a. smoke   b. eat junk food
    c. drink alcohol   d. sleep less than 8 hours

4. What bad habit do the least number of students have?
    a. smoking   b. eating junk food
    c. drinking alcohol   d. sleeping less than 8 hours

LESSON ⬤1 What skills do you have?

GOAL ■ Identify skills and characteristics

A. Write job descriptions for each of the job titles listed below.

Job title	Description
cashier	rings up purchases
administrative assistant	
architect	
assembler	
contractor	
homemaker	
restaurant manager	
teacher	
bank teller	
soccer coach	

B. Write job titles for each description listed below.

Job title	Description
mail carrier	delivers mail
	fights fires
	writes about the news
	repairs cars
	answers phones
	plays an instrument in an orchestra or band
	builds homes

C. Study the chart.

Restrictive Adjective Clauses	
Subject	**Restrictive adjective clause**
A homemaker is a person	**who takes care of a home and a family.**
The job	**(that) I really want** is in Texas.
A person	**that builds homes** is a contractor.
The place	**where she works** is near her home.

- Restrictive adjective clauses give essential information about the noun they refer to. They cannot be omitted without losing the meaning of the sentence.
- A relative pronoun (*that, which, who[m], whose, when, where*) that is the object of the adjective clause can be omitted.

D. Underline the restrictive adjective clauses in each sentence.

1. My company is looking for someone <u>who can maintain and repair computers.</u>

2. This is a new position that opened up recently.

3. There are several skills that this person must have.

4. The ideal candidate is a person who is self-motivated and works well alone.

5. Is this a job that you think you might enjoy, or do you prefer working with people?

6. There is another job that might interest you in our downtown office.

7. We also have an office in the town where you live.

8. I think there are several jobs that are suitable for you.

9. You are just the type of person that we are looking for.

E. Go back and cross out the relative pronouns that can be omitted in Exercise D.

EXAMPLE: 3. There are several skills ~~that~~ this person must have.

F. Combine the two sentences into one sentence using a restrictive adjective clause.

1. Carlos heard about a job. The job was advertised on the Internet.

   Carlos heard about a job that was advertised on the Internet.

2. He sent his resume to the address. The address was posted on the website.

   _____

3. The company is looking for an employee. The employee is fluent in Spanish.

   _____

4. Carlos filled out the application. The personnel manager sent him the application.

   _____

5. He has an interview Monday with the supervisor. The supervisor is in charge of the position.

   _____

6. Carlos is sure he has the qualifications. The company is looking for the qualifications.

   _____

7. He is looking forward to meeting the woman. The woman might be his future supervisor.

   _____

8. Carlos received a phone call that night. The phone call was that he got the job.

   _____

9. This company is a place. He has always wanted to work for this company.

   _____

G. Look back at the jobs and descriptions from exercises A and B. Write seven sentences with adjective clauses.

1. _A cashier is someone who rings up purchases._

2. _____

3. _____

4. _____

5. _____

6. _____

7. _____

LESSON ② Looking for a job

GOAL ■ Conduct a job search

A. Think about the job you have now. (If you are student or a homemaker, that is your job.) Complete the chart with information about your job.

Information about my job	
Job title	
Hours	
Days	
Job location	
Benefits	
Required skills	
Required qualifications	

B. Imagine that you are looking for a new job. Answer the questions below.

1. What kind of job would you like to find? _____

2. How much money would you like to make? _____

3. Where would you like to work (ex: outside, in an office, in a hospital)? _____

C. Imagine you ask a partner the same questions. Write his/her possible answers.

1. What kind of job would you like to find? _____

2. How much money would you like to make? _____

3. Where would you like to work (ex: outside, in an office, in a hospital)? _____

D. **Study the chart on generalizations.**

Generalizations	
Example	**Explanation**
Experience is needed for this job. ~~The~~ experience is needed for this job. Classes begin next week at school. ~~The~~ classes begin next week at school. Strong communication skills are desirable. ~~The~~ strong communication skills are desirable.	To make a generalization about the subject of a sentence, do not use an article.
I don't have <u>the</u> experience to be <u>the</u> cashier. <u>The</u> class I want starts on Tuesday. She has <u>the</u> skills to do <u>the</u> job.	Placing the article *the* in front of a noun makes the noun specific.

E. **Write *the* for specific nouns. Write Ø if a generalization is being made.**

1. I think I have ____the____ skills for that job.

2. It's necessary to send _____ references with your resume.

3. Where are _____ letters of recommendation he sent?

4. Do you have _____ strong communication skills?

5. I'm going to be late for _____ meeting.

6. Where are _____ computers you want me to repair?

7. _____ knowledge of accounting is helpful if you want to be an administrative assistant.

8. You don't have _____ qualifications they are looking for.

9. They want someone who is good with _____ people.

10. _____ classes that I'm taking started last night.

11. I couldn't find a job in _____ ads that I was reading.

F. Complete the paragraph with *the* for specific nouns and *Ø* for generalizations.

What are (1) __the__ steps you should follow to get a good job? First, you might want to look on (2) _____ Internet. You'll find (3) _____ jobs listed there. When you find a job that sounds interesting, look at (4) _____ job requirements. Is (5) _____ experience necessary? Do you have to have (6) _____ knowledge of computers? You should determine if you have (7) _____ training and (8) _____ skills that (9) _____ company is looking for. You should also think about what is more important to you in life: (10) _____ money or (11) _____ happiness? Will (12) _____ job give you (13) _____ opportunity to achieve your goals?

If you decide to apply for one of (14) _____ jobs, you should send a resume to (15) _____ address provided in (16) _____ ad. After a week, you should call (17) _____ company office to ask for an interview. You might want to practice for (18) _____ interview. Remember, (19) _____ first impressions are important. Show (20) _____ confidence at your interview! I hope you have (21) _____ good luck!

G. Write generalizations based on the information given.

1. (confidence / will help you / work / get)

   Confidence will help you get work. _____

2. (job / benefits / I'm looking / for / like health insurance)

   _____

3. (decided / I / to apply / have / jobs / near my home / for)

   _____

4. (me / hours / good / for / afternoon / will be)

   _____

5. (get / a / computer class / will help me / job)

   _____

H. Write two generalizations that describe how you feel about a job that you're looking for.

1. _____

2. _____

LESSON ③ Resumes

GOAL ■ Write a resume

A. Read Tanya's resume and answer the questions below.

Tanya Pitre

6798 Monte Vista Road • Pasadena, CA 91105
tpitre@loa.net • (626) 555-3839

EDUCATION

2012–2015	Pasadena City College AA Business Administration
2010–2012	Pasadena Community Education Center Computer Classes (Word, Excel, PowerPoint) Writing Classes

EXPERIENCE

2013–present	City Center, Pasadena, CA Office Assistant
2010–2013	Santa Anita Mall Retail Clerk
2008–2010	Harvey's Burgers Cashier

1. What school did she attend first? _____

2. What did she study at Pasadena Community Education Center? _____

3. What did she get her degree in? _____

4. How many jobs has she had? _____

5. What is the first job listed on her resume? _____

6. Does she still have that job? _____ How can you tell?

B. Study the chart.

Past Perfect Tense: Forms			
	Subject	***Had/Hadn't***	**Past participle**	**Complement**

	Subject	*Had/Hadn't*	Past participle	Complement
Statement	I I	**had** **hadn't**	**sent** **received**	my resume in May. a response before today.

	Wh- word	*Had/Hadn't*	Subject	Past participle	Complement
Question	Why	**had** **had**	she you	**had** **hired**	an interview before? him?

• The past perfect tense is formed with ***had/had not (hadn't)*** + past participle.
• Subject pronouns (except ***it***) can contract with ***had: I'd, you'd, he'd, she'd, we'd, they'd***

C. Circle the correct past perfect sentence.

1. (I had finished school by 2010.)/ I have finished school by 2010.

2. She had never be to an interview before. / She had never been to an interview before.

3. He said he had never worked as a cashier. / He said he had never work as a cashier.

4. Before last month, we'd never written a resume. / Before last month, we're never written a resume.

5. Santiago'd studied hard to become a lawyer. / Santiago had studied hard to become a lawyer.

6. Had you worked in an office before? / Had you working in an office before?

7. It'd the best job I had ever had. / It had been the best job I had ever had.

8. Why Luc had had so many jobs? / Why had Luc had so many jobs?

9. Had they enjoyed assembling computers? / Had enjoyed they assembling computers?

D. Write the past perfect tense of each verb below.

1. work	*had worked*	2. live	
3. do		4. be	
5. look		6. complete	
7. apply		8. find	
9. call		10. get	

E. Complete each sentence with the past perfect tense of the verb in parentheses. Use contractions where possible.

1. (find) Cristina asked if I *'d found* _____ a new hobby.

2. (practice) Raj _____ interviewing for the job.

3. (not / enclose) Linh _____ a resume with her application.

4. (never / have) We _____ a performance review before last week.

5. (provide) I _____ letters of recommendation already.

6. (said) They _____ that they were willing to accept responsibility.

7. (not / find) Chan _____ information about the company until today.

8. (look) You _____ forward to discussing job opportunities.

9. (be) She _____ friendly and patient with the customers.

F. Write past perfect sentences using the information given in parentheses.

1. (Tanya / write / her resume / before she called the manager)

   Tanya had written her resume before she called the manager.

2. (Tanya / attend / Pasadena City College / before 2008)

   _____

3. (work / she / as an office assistant / before)

   _____

4. (Tanya / take / computer classes / before she got her AA)

   _____

5. (she / go / to Pasadena Community Education Center / first)

   _____

G. Think about information you would put on your own resume and write sentences using the past perfect tense.

1. *I had worked as a bank teller first.*

2. _____

3. _____

4. _____

5. _____

LESSON 4 Cover letters

GOAL ■ Write an e-mail

A. Read the advertisement. Is this a job you would be good at? Why or why not?

HELP WANTED

Company: Home Styles
Company Description: A company that makes and sells furniture
Job Title: Customer Service Representative
Job Description: Answering phones and helping customers. Good verbal and personal skills a plus. Should be highly motivated, dependable, and a hard worker. Willing to train.

B. Read the e-mail that Elise wrote to the manager of the furniture company and answer the questions that follow.

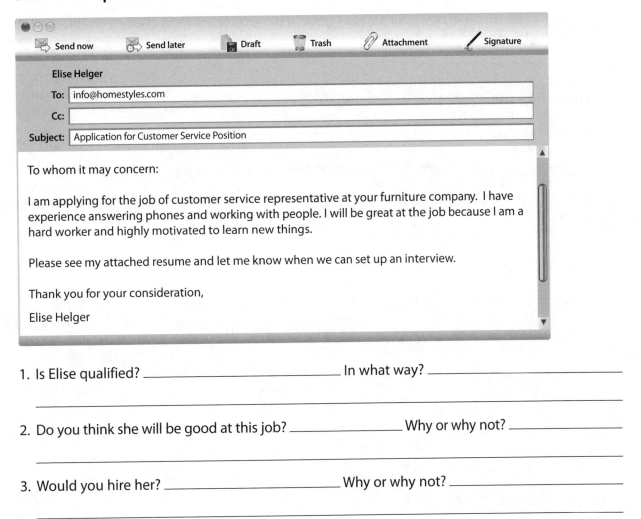

Send now   Send later   Draft   Trash   Attachment   Signature

Elise Helger

To: info@homestyles.com

Cc:

Subject: Application for Customer Service Position

To whom it may concern:

I am applying for the job of customer service representative at your furniture company. I have experience answering phones and working with people. I will be great at the job because I am a hard worker and highly motivated to learn new things.

Please see my attached resume and let me know when we can set up an interview.

Thank you for your consideration,

Elise Helger

1. Is Elise qualified? _____ In what way? _____

_____

2. Do you think she will be good at this job? _____ Why or why not? _____

_____

3. Would you hire her? _____ Why or why not? _____

_____

C. Study the chart.

Past Perfect Tense: Uses	
Example	**Rule**
Before I got my job as a computer technician, I **had worked** as a delivery person.	To show that an event happened before another event in the past.
She **had** already **prepared** her resume **when** the company called her for an interview.	To show that an event happened before the verb in the *when* clause.
After I **had written** my resume and cover letter, I realized it was too late to send it.	With *after*, to show that something was finished before another event in the past.
There were a lot of job applicants **because** the company **had posted** the position on the Internet.	After *because*, to show a prior reason.
Many of the employees **had never worked** in sales **before** this job.	With *never . . . before*, in relation to a past event.
My supervisor thanked me for all the hard work **that** I **had done.**	In a *who/that/which* clause to show a past event.

D. Underline the event that happened first.

1. When I called her, <u>she had already left for her meeting.</u>

2. Because he hadn't received his degree yet, he didn't apply for the job.

3. She'd had the dry cleaning business for three years when she decided to open her own store.

4. Before you came to the United States, you had studied to be a teacher.

5. He found out that there were no jobs available after he had filled out the application.

6. This morning they finished repairing all the broken computers that I had given them yesterday.

7. We had interviewed many applicants before we found the right person for the job.

E. Complete each sentence with the past perfect tense of the verb in parentheses.

1. (have) I couldn't sleep last night because I _____ had had _____ a bad day at work.

2. (never / enjoy) Mike _____ his job before now.

3. (finish) After I _____ the interview, I met my future coworkers.

4. (save) Because you _____ your money, you were able to open your own business.

5. (give) They didn't like the new duties that their supervisor _____ them.

6. (not / go) Yuko was upset because her interview _____ well.

7. (already / write) Before we came to the United States, we _____ our resumes.

8. (not / make) He didn't get the job because he _____ a good impression.

9. (handle) I _____ customer complaints before I became the supervisor.

F. Think about your own job and write different sentences based on each situation below. Look at the examples from the chart in Exercise C.

1. (show that an event happened after another event, using *when*)

   I had already interviewed for the job when the manager called me._____

2. (show that one event happened before another)

   _____

3. (show that an event happened after another using *when*)

   _____

4. (using *after*, show that something was finished before another event)

   _____

5. (use *because* to show a prior reason)

   _____

6. (use *never...before*, in relation to a past event)

   _____

7. (use *that* to show a past event)

   _____

GOAL ■ Prepare for a job interview

A. **Write about your employment history. Complete the charts below.**

Job titles

First job I had	Second job I had

Company names

First company I worked at	Second company I worked at

Job titles

First job I interviewed for	Second job I interviewed for

City names

First city I worked in	Second city I worked in

B. **Combine the two ideas in the charts by filling in the blanks below. Put the second idea first.**

1. Before I was a _____*chef,*_____ I had been _____*a line cook.*_____

2. Before I was a _____, I had been a _____.

3. Before I worked at _____, I had worked at _____.

4. Before I interviewed for _____, I had interviewed for _____.

5. Before I worked in _____, I had worked in _____.

C. Study the chart.

Past Perfect Tense with Simple Past	
Example	**Explanation**
Before Ranjit **got** the job as a repairperson, (simple past) he **had worked** as an assembler. (past perfect)	Use the past perfect for the event that happened first in the past. Use the simple past for the event that happened second.
When she **arrived** at the interview, (simple past) the interviewer **had** already **read** her résumé . (past perfect)	

now

past ◄- -|- - - - - ► future

1. Ranjit had worked
2. the interviewer had read

Ranjit got the job
she arrived

D. Read each sentence and decide what happened second. Underline it.

1. I had moved to Telluride <u>before my sister moved there.</u>

2. I quit my old job because my supervisor hadn't given me enough responsibility.

3. I applied for a new job that I had seen on the Internet.

4. When I arrived in Houston, I had already researched the company.

5. I had already sent a resume when I got a call for an interview.

6. Because I had practiced what to say and do many times, I felt a little more prepared for the interview.

E. Complete the sentences with either the simple past tense or the past perfect tense of the verbs in parentheses.

1. I ____had lived____ (live) in Miami for two years before I ____moved____ (move) to Houston.

2. I _____ (never / be) so nervous about something before.

3. When I _____ (get) to the interview, the interviewer _____ (already / read) my recommendations and my transcripts.

4. She _____ (ask) me why I _____ (be) unhappy at my last job.

5. I _____ (explain) that I _____ (not / be) completely unhappy.

6. Before I _____ (leave) my old job, my former supervisor _____ (even / write) a recommendation for me.

7. He _____ (say) that I _____ (be) hardworking and self-motivated.

8. Unfortunately, he _____ (not / have) the opportunity to really take advantage of my skills.

9. By the time I _____ (leave) the interview, I _____ (make) a good impression.

10. Last night, I _____ (find out) that I _____ (get) the job.

11. I _____ (never / feel) so excited and happy before!

F. Write past perfect sentences about your employment history using the information you wrote in Exercise A.

1. (had) _I had had a job as a food server before I had a job as a cashier._____

2. (had) _____

_____

3. (work at) _____

_____

4. (interview) _____

_____

5. (work in) _____

_____

PRACTICE TEST

A. Look at the resume and choose the best answer.

Eric Jones

ericjones.4444@joh.edu • (714) 555-7522

EXPERIENCE	
Santa Ana College, School of Continuing Education Santa Ana, California **Teacher's Assistant**	2013–present
California State University Long Beach Long Beach, California **Learning Lab Assistant**	2010–2013
Orange Coast College Costa Mesa, California **Learning Lab Assistant**	2010–2013
CGB Aerospace Garden Grove, California **Technology Repairperson** Developed specialized curriculum and taught Workplace English to aerospace employees.	2000–2010

1. What does Eric do for work?

   a. He is a teacher.

   c. He is a lab assistant.

   b. He is a technology repairperson.

   d. He is a teacher's assistant.

2. What job did he have the longest?

   a. repairperson

   c. teaching assistant

   b. lab assistant

   d. He had all the jobs for the same amount of time.

3. Where was he a learning lab assistant?

   a. Santa Ana College

   c. California State University Long Beach

   b. Orange Coast College

   d. both b and c

4. What do three of his workplaces have in common?

   a. He had the same job at three places.

   c. He did repairs at three places.

   b. They are all art schools.

   d. They are all higher education institutions.

LESSON ① She's late, isn't she?

GOAL ◼ Identify appropriate and inappropriate workplace behavior

A. **Look at the list of workplace behavior and decide which is acceptable and which is unacceptable. Complete the table. Add a few of your own ideas.**

Workplace Behavior

Send e-mail to a friend

Take paper home from the copy room

Ask your manager for help

Arrive early

Call in sick

Show up late from break

Acceptable	Unacceptable

B. **Answer the following questions about yourself with *Yes* or *No*.**

1. You show up for work on time, don't you? _____

2. You asked for help on your resume, didn't you? _____

3. You are always late for class, aren't you? _____

4. You aren't looking for a new job, are you? _____

5. You will go to college, won't you? _____

6. You e-mail at work, don't you? _____

C. Study the chart.

Tag Questions			
Tense	Affirmative statement	Negative tag question	Answer
simple present	You work,	**don't** you?	Yes, I do. / No, I don't.
present continuous	You are working,	**aren't** you?	Yes, I am. / No, I'm not.
future	You will work,	**won't** you?	Yes, I will. / No, I won't.
simple past	They talked,	**didn't** they?	Yes, they did. / No, they didn't.
past continuous	They were talking,	**weren't** they?	Yes, they were. / No, they weren't.
present perfect	They have talked,	**haven't** they?	Yes, they have. / No, they haven't.
past perfect	They had talked,	**hadn't** they?	Yes, they had. / No, they hadn't.

- Tag questions are used to check if something is true or to ask for agreement.
- A tag question uses an auxiliary verb + a subject pronoun.
- The tag question uses the same tense as the main verb.
- A tag question can consist of a negative tag statement and an affirmative tag question.
    You aren't a new employee, **are** you?
    She won't apply for the job, **will** she?
- Negative tags are usually contracted.

D. Match the tag questions to the statements.

1. We got raises, ___e___

2. They were informed of the problem, _____

3. Gilberto didn't do a good job, _____

4. The company was offering stock options, _____

5. I haven't been late for any meetings, _____

6. Sara had worked hard, _____

7. They arrived a few minutes late to work, _____

8. You haven't been working from home, _____

9. I was at that meeting, _____

10. We had increased the company's profitability, _____

11. She has taken more responsibility, _____

a. hadn't she?

b. weren't they?

c. wasn't it?

d. didn't they?

e. didn't we?

f. have you?

g. hasn't she?

h. hadn't we?

i. wasn't I?

j. have I?

k. did he?

E. Circle the correct tag question for each statement.

1. He will ask for a raise, doesn't he / <u>won't he</u>?
2. You send personal e-mails, <u>don't you</u> / aren't you?
3. She is coming back early from break, <u>won't she</u> / isn't she?
4. We won't be late, <u>will we</u> / won't we?
5. He meets with his boss every day, does he / <u>doesn't he</u>?
6. I don't have time to shower before work, <u>don't I</u> / do I?
7. Packages are left with the receptionist, <u>aren't they</u> / isn't they?

F. Add a tag question to each statement. Then, answer the question.

1. You are buying supplies, _____aren't you?_____   (yes) _____Yes, I am._____

2. I'm getting a raise, _____   (yes) _____

3. Yolanda had compiled a portfolio, _____   (yes) _____

4. You have experience, _____   (no) _____

5. They bought the supplies, _____   (yes) _____

6. I was paid for overtime hours, _____   (no) _____

7. The copier isn't broken, _____   (yes) _____

8. She will have a new office, _____   (yes) _____

9. The letter has been signed, _____   (no) _____

10. It won't increase productivity, _____   (no) _____

11. They didn't miss work, _____   (yes) _____

G. Imagine you are interviewing someone for a job at your restaurant. Write four questions you would ask them. Use tag questions.

1. You know how to make desserts, don't you?

2. _____

3. _____

4. _____

5. _____

LESSON **2** The note was written by Jim

GOAL ■ Identify workplace actions

A. Think about the job you have now. (If you are a student or a homemaker, that is your job.) What are things that happen at your workplace? Write sentences.

1. <u>Cooks prepare food</u> . or <u>Employees assemble computers</u> .

2. _____

3. _____

4. _____

5. _____

B. Many items are created by people with particular skills. Write a short sentence that explains how the item was produced and who produced it. Use the verb in parentheses.

Item	Description
1. wedding cake	(made) <u>The cake was made by a baker.</u>
2. broken window	(fix) _____
3. poem	(write) _____
4. laundry	(done) _____
5. model airplane	(made) _____
6. painting	(made) _____
7. necklace	(made) _____
8. men's suit	(made) _____
9. wooden table	(made) _____
10. computer	(made) _____

C. Study the chart on the passive voice.

Passive Voice: Form					
	Subject	*Be*	**Past participle**	*By* + person/thing	
Statement	A meeting	is	held		every day.
	The orders	were	sent	by Jim	yesterday.
	Be	**Subject**	**Past participle**	*By* + person/thing	
Yes/No Question	Is	a meeting	held		every day?
	Were	the orders	sent	by Jim	yesterday?

• Use the passive voice to emphasize the object of the action or when the doer of the action is unknown or unimportant.
• Use the passive voice with **by** if the doer of the action is mentioned.

D. Circle the subject and underline the passive verb in each sentence.

1. (Those papers) <u>were filed</u> last night.

2. The orders were sent yesterday.

3. The server was put next to the copy machine.

4. The whole crew was sent to a training class in Atlanta.

5. The planes were built by that new aerospace company.

6. A meeting was held about the changes in benefits.

7. He was given a receipt.

8. The employees were laid off due to budget cuts.

9. The package was mailed a week ago.

10. The gifts were wrapped by the customer service department.

11. The sprinklers were repaired last week.

12. The new lights were installed by the handyman.

13. They were charged for the change in paint color.

E. **Unscramble the words to write statements and questions in the passive voice.**

1. a / given / was / promotion / Lynn / .

    <u>Lynn was given a promotion.</u>

2. was / wrong / the / given / the / change / customer / .

    _____

3. the / receipt / given / was / he / ?

    _____

4. problem / many / affected / are / the / people / by / .

    _____

5. fired / job / Monica / from / was / her / ?

    _____

6. to / are / work / allowed / flex-time / you / ?

    _____

7. the / written / is / letter / ?

    _____

8. the / taken / the / were / closet / supplies / from / ?

    _____

F. **Write passive sentences about things that happen in your home.**

1. windows / wash   <u>The windows are washed once a month.</u>

2. dinner / cook   _____

3. clothes / wash   _____

4. beds / made   _____

5. lights / turn on   _____

6. yard / clean   _____

7. groceries / buy   _____

GOAL ■ Communicate problems to a supervisor

A. **Read about a problem you might have at work, at home, or at school. Brainstorm your own problem. Write the problem below.**

My problem:

Work: My paycheck is wrong. I worked more hours than I got paid for.

Home: The refrigerator is broken. The food in the freezer isn't staying frozen.

School: I got put in a class I didn't register for.

_____

_____

B. **Answer the questions about your problem.**

1. Who will you talk to? _____

2. How will you talk to them? (e.g., calmly, quietly, etc.) _____

3. What will you say to them? _____

_____

4. How will you suggest the problem be solved? _____

_____

C. **Write out how you would like the conversation to go.**

You: _____

_____ : _____

You: _____

_____ : _____

You: _____

_____ : _____

You: _____

_____ : _____

D. Study the chart.

Passive Voice: Overview of Tenses	
Tense	**Passive (*be* + past participle)**
simple present	The decision **is made.**
present continuous	The decision **is being made.**
future	The decision **will be made.** / The decision **is going to be made.**
simple past	The decision **was made.**
past continuous	The decision **was being made.**
present perfect	The decision **has been made.**
past perfect	The decision **had been made.**
• In the passive voice, the past participle is the same for all tenses. Only the form of *be* changes. • An adverb can be placed between the auxiliary verb and the past participle. The decision was **already** made.	

E. Change the sentence to the indicated tenses: *Our supervisor was told about the problem.*

1. (past perfect)   Our supervisor had been told about the problem.

2. (present perfect)   _____

3. (present continuous) _____

4. (future)   _____

5. (past continuous)   _____

6. (simple past)   _____

Change the sentence to the indicated tenses: *The problem was solved.*

7. (present perfect)   _____

8. (present continuous) _____

9. (future)   _____

10. (past continuous)   _____

11. (simple present)   _____

12. (past perfect)   _____

F. Complete each sentence using the verb in parentheses in the indicated tense.

1. (present perfect: leave) A package _____ has been left _____ in your office.

2. (future: finish) The work _____ tomorrow.

3. (past continuous: order) The right supplies _____.

4. (past perfect: give) I _____ a promotion three times.

5. (present perfect: speak) He _____ to twice about being late for work.

6. (simple past: receive) The phone call _____ at 3:00 p.m. by Fernando.

7. (past perfect: pay) He _____ for overtime hours.

8. (past continuous: make) The copies _____ on the office copier.

9. (future: fire) You _____ if you take home company supplies.

10. (present continuous: solve) The problem _____ by the supervisor.

11. (future: inform) The human resources director _____.

G. Write two passive voice sentences about each situation below. Use your imagination.

The ATM machine gave me the incorrect cash. I had to go into the bank to talk to the bank manager.

1. _____

2. _____

My teacher forgot to record my test scores in her book. I had to stay and talk to her after class.

1. _____

2. _____

I didn't get a promotion at work. I e-mailed my supervisor to see if he could explain why.

1. _____

2. _____

H. Think back to the problem you wrote about in exercises A and B. Write three sentences about the solution using passive voice.

1. The refrigerator will be fixed. _____

2. _____

3. _____

4. _____

LESSON **4** **What should you do?**

GOAL ■ Make ethical decisions

A. Look at each situation. Why do you think passive voice was used? Write your ideas below each situation.

1. The computer was stolen.

   _____

2. The chef was given the secret recipe.

   _____

3. Two hundred copies were made last night after hours.

   _____

4. Toilet paper was taken from the supply closet.

   _____

5. The information was leaked to the public.

   _____

B. Look at each statement and rewrite it in the passive voice.

1. Someone ate the last piece of cake.

   _____

2. This morning, 10,000 people ran the marathon.

   _____

3. Amelio jumped the fence.

   _____

4. Kenji left the television on last night.

   _____

C. Study the chart.

Active to Passive Voice	
Active	**Passive**
Someone stole the computer.	The computer has been stolen.
The chef gave his brother the secret recipe.	The secret recipe was given to his brother.
Will someone tell the owner about the problem?	Will the owner be told about the problem?
• To make an active sentence passive, switch the subject and the object, and change the verb to the correct tense of **be** + past participle. • Do not use **by** if the doer of the action is not known.	

D. Write *A* if the sentence uses the active voice. Write *P* if the sentence uses the passive voice.

1. __P__ The problem was already being discussed last month.

2. _____ She had finished her work by noon.

3. _____ Were you going to negotiate a raise?

4. _____ Nick has been given a new office.

5. _____ You will be informed of my decision later.

6. _____ I should have received an e-mail from her.

7. _____ Are stock options now being offered?

8. _____ Was the package paid for by your boss?

9. _____ We might also get more vacation time.

E. Change six passive voice sentences to active voice. Add a subject if necessary.

1. They discussed the problem last month.

2. _____

3. _____

4. _____

5. _____

6. _____

F. **Change the sentences from active to passive voice.**

1. Someone had sent suspicious e-mails from this office.

   Suspicious e-mails had been sent from this office.

2. Mr. Lee called an emergency meeting at 10:00 a.m.

   _____

3. Someone had used the Internet illegally.

   _____

4. Someone was sending secret company information to another company.

   _____

5. Mr. Lee called the police to investigate the situation.

   _____

6. The police were interviewing everyone in the office.

   _____

7. They are going to check all our computers.

   _____

8. Mr. Lee will ask us to help solve the problem.

   _____

9. Unfortunately, the company never found the person who did it.

   _____

G. **Look back at the situations in Exercise A. Rewrite each situation using active voice with the subjects given below.**

1. (the night manager)

   The night manager stole the computer.

2. (an employee from a competing restaurant)

   _____

3. (the cleaning crew)

   _____

4. (the vandals who broke into the building)

   _____

5. (an upper-level manager)

   _____

LESSON **5** A raise

GOAL ■ Ask for a raise

A. Have you ever asked for a promotion or raise at work? Think of some reasons why people deserve promotions or raises. Use the verbs in the box to write your ideas.

bring	sell	buy	offer	show	take
teach	write	build	make	find	

He sells a lot of products to his customers. She taught her coworkers how to use the computer.

_____

_____

_____

_____

B. Why do you think you deserve a raise or promotion at work? Or why do you think you deserve to move up to the next level in school? Write a paragraph to convince your supervisor or instructor.

_____

_____

_____

_____

_____

C. Study the chart.

Verbs with Two Objects	
Example	**Explanation**
My boss gave **me a promotion.** I gave **Tito the mail.**	Many verbs can have both a direct object and an indirect object.
The cashier gave the receipt **to me.** Sam bought a computer **for her.**	When the indirect object comes last, the preposition *to* or *for* is usually used.
I sent **Ana the e-mail.** I sent **the e-mail to Ana.**	With many verbs, either the direct or the indirect object can come first.
Can you **explain the plan to me**? ~~Can you **explain me the plan**?~~	With the verbs *say, describe, suggest,* and *explain*, the indirect object *cannot* come first.
A package was given to Chan. **Chan was given** a package.	With passive sentences with two objects, two structures are possible.

- *To* is used with *bring, give, lend, offer, pay, read, sell, send, show, take, teach, tell, write.*
- *For* is used with *build, buy, do, find, get, make, prepare.*
- No preposition is used with *ask, cost, wish.*

D. Circle the correct sentence.

1. (Nothing was sent to me by e-mail.) / Nothing to me was sent by e-mail.

2. Can you describe me the problem? / Can you describe the problem to me?

3. I took the report to Mrs. Louis. / I took to Mrs. Louis the report.

4. Your portfolio was shown to the director. / To the director was shown your portfolio.

5. They give me good benefits. / They give to me good benefits.

6. Would you explain him the opportunities? / Would you explain the opportunities to him?

7. A promotion to Silvio has been given. / Silvio has been given a promotion.

8. To me, the supervisor showed the results. / The supervisor showed me the results.

9. Could you explain the solution to me? / Could you explain me the solution?

E. Change the order of objects in each sentence. If the order cannot be changed, write *No change.*

1. Will you give the promotion to me?   _Will you give me the promotion?_

2. She sent me an urgent message about my raise.   _____

3. Andre has been offered a great job.   _____

4. I found a job for my coworker.   _____

5. Will you describe your position to me?   _____

6. Forms for her raise were brought to her boss.   _____

F. Write sentences using the verb and two objects given. Write each sentence two ways if possible.

1. (show / computer program / me) _He showed me the computer program. He showed the computer_

   program to me.

2. (give / application / me) _____

   _____

3. (prepare / presentation / boss) _____

   _____

4. (write / proposal / her) _____

   _____

5. (read / fine print / him) _____

   _____

G. Look at the sentences in Exercise B. Change the sentences to include two objects.

1. _I taught my coworkers the safety standards._

2. _____

3. _____

4. _____

PRACTICE TEST

A. Read the conversation and choose the best answer.

Tiffany: Excuse me, Eric, can I talk to you for a second?

Manager: Sure, what's up, Tiffany?

Tiffany: Well, I'm having a problem with the server schedule. It seems that so many people asked for certain days off that I don't have enough servers to work next weekend.

Manager: Yes, that can be problem. That's why we have the "Days Off Requests" dated. You need to put the requests in order by date. The first people who turned in their requests can have the day off, but if you need to schedule people, the servers who requested later can't have the day off.

Tiffany: OK, that makes sense. So, what do I tell the people who don't get their requested day off?

Manager: Tell them to reread the manual they received when they were hired. It clearly explains the policies and procedures for requesting days off and tells them that just because they request a certain day off doesn't mean they will get it.

Tiffany: Got it. Thanks, Eric.

Manager: No problem.

1. What is the problem?

   a. Servers didn't read the manual they were given when they were hired.

   b. Too many people requested the same day off.

   c. The restaurant needs to hire more servers.

   d. Servers forgot to fill out the "Days Off Request."

2. What does Tiffany say to get the manager's attention?

   a. Excuse me.   b. Can you help me?

   c. I'm having a problem.   d. a and c

3. What does the manager say to show he understands the problem?

   a. "Sure, what's up Tiffany?"   b. "It clearly explains the policies and procedures."

   c. "I don't understand the problem."   d. "Yes, that can be a problem."

4. What does the manager suggest Tiffany do to solve the problem?

   a. Put the requests in order by date.   b. Remind servers to reread their manuals.

   c. both a and b   d. neither a nor b

LESSON **1** Solving problems

GOAL ■ Interpret civic responsibilities

A. **Think about the rules in your classroom and answer the questions below by putting a check (✓) under *Yes* or *No*.**

	Yes	No
1. Are you allowed to talk in class?	_____	_____
2. Are you supposed to do your homework every night?	_____	_____
3. Are you required to buy books for your class?	_____	_____
4. Are you permitted to eat during class?	_____	_____
5. Is your teacher supposed to correct your homework?	_____	_____
6. Are you allowed to drink water in class?	_____	_____

B. **Imagine you are the teacher of one of the classes below and you have to set the rules for your class. Write the rules.**

Class Choices: Woodworking   Cooking   Swimming   Target Practice

Class: _____

Rules

1. _____

2. _____

3. _____

4. _____

5. _____

6. _____

C. Study the chart.

Supposed to, Required to, and Allowed/Permitted to	
Example	**Explanation**
You are **supposed to** return the jury summons. You are **not supposed to** tear up the form.	*(Not) supposed to* is a reminder of a legal obligation or a rule.
You are **required to** have a driver's license to drive. You are **not required to** be an organ donor.	*Required to* shows legal obligation. *Not required to* shows no legal obligation.
You are **allowed/permitted to** smoke outside. You are **not allowed/permitted to** smoke inside.	*Allowed/permitted to* shows permission. *Not allowed/permitted to* shows something is against the rules.
• The verb *be* is used with *supposed to, required to*, and *allowed/permitted to.* • Use the base form of a verb after *supposed to, required to,* and *allowed/permitted to.*	

D. Match the underlined expressions in the sentences below with the explanations.

a. legal obligation or rule   b. no legal obligation   c. permission   d. against the rules

1. __d__ Non-citizens are <u>not allowed to</u> vote.

2. _____ Citizens are <u>not required to</u> vote.

3. _____ Non-citizens are <u>permitted to</u> attend local town meetings.

4. _____ Anyone is <u>allowed to</u> voice his or her opinion at these meetings.

5. _____ Non-citizens are <u>not permitted to</u> run for public office.

6. _____ Everyone is <u>supposed to</u> file an income tax return.

7. _____ You're <u>not supposed to</u> throw it away.

8. _____ You are <u>required to</u> report interest from savings on your return.

9. _____ If you're married, you are <u>allowed to</u> file a joint return or a separate return.

E. Answer each question using the words in parentheses.

1. Can I get a driver's license? (yes / allowed to)

   <u>Yes, you are allowed to get a driver's license.</u>

2. Can I drive a car without a license? (no / not / permitted to)

   _____

3. Do I have to take a written test? (yes / supposed to)

   _____

4. Do I have to study the driver's handbook first? (no / not / required to)

   _____

5. Do I have to fill out an application for the road test? (yes / required to)

   _____

6. Can I talk on the phone during the road test? (no / not / allowed to)

   _____

7. Can I drive if my license is suspended? (no / not / allowed to)

   _____

8. Do I have to take a driving class to learn how to drive? (yes / supposed to)

   _____

9. Can I take the driving test before I pass the written test? (no / not / allowed to)

   _____

F. Write sentences about rules in your classroom using the expressions given.

1. (allowed to) <u>We are allowed to work on our homework with other students.</u>

2. (permitted to) _____

3. (supposed to) _____

4. (not allowed to) _____

5. (not supposed to) _____

6. (required to) _____

LESSON ② A driver's license and jury duty

GOAL ■ Apply for a driver's license and respond to a jury summons

A. **Imagine that you are going to get a driver's license. Put the steps below in the correct order (1–6).**

_____ Get picture taken.

_____ Take and pass written test.

_____ Receive license in the mail.

_____ Study for the written test.

_____ Take and pass the driving test.

_____ Practice driving.

B. **Imagine that you have received a jury summons in the mail. Put the steps in the correct order (1–4).**

_____ Report to the court for jury duty.

_____ Mail the jury summons in.

_____ Fill out the jury summons.

_____ Answer questions from the judge and the lawyers.

C. **Answer the following questions.**

1. Who makes you do your homework? _____

2. Who lets you get a driver's license? _____

3. Who makes you fill out a jury summons? _____

4. Who has you sit at a desk in your classroom? _____

5. Who makes you come to class? _____

6. Who makes you stop at traffic lights when they are red? _____

7. Who lets you choose which candidate to vote for in an election?_____

8. Who makes you pay income tax? _____

D. Study the chart.

Causative Verbs	
Example	**Explanation**
The government **makes you register** and **insure** your car. The court **makes you fill out** a jury summons.	*Make* means *force* or *require*.
The police **lets you drive** in the carpool lane if you have more than one person in your car. The court **lets you opt out** of jury duty if you have small children to care for.	*Let* means *permit*.
The DMV **has you take** a written test before you get your license. Some courts **have you call** in before you report for jury service.	*Have* means *give a job or task to someone*.
• *Make, let,* and *have* are called causative verbs because one person causes or allows another to do something. • The sentence structure is: causative verb + object + base form.	

E. Find the mistake in each sentence. Then, rewrite the sentence correctly.

1. My parents are letting buy me a car.

   My parents are letting me buy a car.

2. But first they are making me all the money earn.

   _____

3. Once I earn enough money, they will letting me look for and buy the car.

   _____

4. They will have me registering the car in my name.

   _____

5. My dad is make me get insurance.

   _____

6. Then, they will let me to drive wherever I want.

   _____

7. If I get a speeding ticket, they will me have give them my keys for a month.

   _____

F.   Choose the best word in parentheses to complete each sentence.

1. The government (has / makes / lets) you fill out a jury summons.

2. Because she doesn't speak English, May (let / had / made) her friend fill out her jury summons.

3. Police officers (let / have / make) you show your license if they stop you for speeding.

4. If you don't agree with a ticket, the government (has / lets / makes) you fight it in court.

5. The judge is (having / letting / making) the jurors keep quiet about the case.

6. I hope the judge (makes / lets / has) us have an hour for lunch.

7. I (make / have / let) my children be home by 10:00 at night since they are driving themselves.

8. The DMV (lets / has / makes) you get another driver's license if you lose yours.

9. You can't (have / make / let) someone get a license if he doesn't want to.

G.   Circle the sentence that is true.

1. Our teacher lets us drink in class. Our teacher doesn't let us drink in class.

2. Our teacher makes us do our homework. Our teacher lets us do our homework.

3. The school lets us buy books. The school doesn't let us buy books.

4. Our teacher has us work in groups. Our teacher doesn't have us work in groups.

5. Our school lets us park in the parking lot. Our school doesn't let us park in the parking lot.

H.   Write sentences about your teacher using the words given.

1. (make) _____

2. (let) _____

3. (have) _____

4. (not, make) _____

5. (not, let) _____

6. (not, have) _____

LESSON ③ Problems in your community

GOAL ■ Communicate opinions about a community problem

A. Brainstorm a list of community problems.

Problems in Our Community

not enough sidewalks

a lot of crime

B. List several of the problems and what solutions you think would work.

Problem	Solution
Potholes	Filling up the potholes

C. Answer the following questions about how you would solve certain community problems.

1. What can be done about too much traffic on the neighborhood streets?

_____

2. What might be done about the overpopulation of pets?

_____

3. What can be done about teenagers driving recklessly?

_____

D. Study the chart.

Gerunds and Infinitives as Subjects	
Example	**Explanation**
Investing time in our community's problems is important. **Finding** solutions as a community is key. **Raising** money isn't easy.	A gerund can be the subject of a sentence.
It is important **to invest** time in our community's problems. It is key **to find** solutions as a community. It isn't easy **to raise** money.	An infinitive phrase is often used with *it* as the subject of a sentence. The meaning is the same as using a gerund subject.
• Gerund and infinitive subjects are followed by a singular verb.	

E. Rewrite each sentence with a gerund as subject.

1. It is necessary to get involved.

   Getting involved is necessary.

2. It takes time to solve community problems.

   _____

3. It won't be easy to get rid of crime.

   _____

4. It will be difficult to make a final decision.

   _____

5. It is very important to improve our public transportation.

   _____

6. It is crucial to take care of homeless people.

   _____

7. It is not a good idea to increase school tuition fees.

   _____

F. Rewrite each sentence so that it uses an infinitive phrase.

1. Being a good citizen is not a requirement.

   It is not a requirement to be a good citizen.

2. Lowering tuition fees is important.

   _____

3. Implementing standards and improving schools might be difficult.

   _____

4. Building new schools will take many years.

   _____

5. Planning for new highways will take many years.

   _____

6. Coming up with a plan to reduce gang violence is very important.

   _____

7. Raising money for new parks and recreation programs should be at the top of our list.

   _____

G. Think back to the problems brainstormed in Exercise A. Write eight sentences (four with gerunds and four with infinitives) about those problems.

Gerunds

1. *Putting in more sidewalks is important.*

2. _____

3. _____

4. _____

5. _____

Infinitives

1. *It will take time to reduce the high crime rate.*

2. _____

3. _____

4. _____

5. _____

GOAL ■ Interpret the electoral process

A. Can you name the following elected officials? Complete the chart.

Title	Name
Mayor of your city	
President of the United States	
Vice President of the United States	
Senator from your state	
Representative from your state	
Student President of your school	

B. Rewrite the following sentences using the word *get*.

1. The president was reelected.

   The president got reelected.

2. The motorist was stopped by a policeman.

   _____

3. The new congressman was voted in.

   _____

4. The old mayor was voted out.

   _____

5. The juror was thrown out by the judge.

   _____

6. The senator was chosen by the majority.

   _____

C. Study the chart.

Passives with *Get*	
Passive with *be*	**Passive with** *get*
Government officials **are elected** by the people.	Government officials **get elected** by the people.
They **aren't** voted in by their peers.	They **don't get** voted in by their peers.
The mayor **was chosen** for his environmental agenda.	The mayor **got chosen** for his environmental agenda.
He **wasn't picked** for his speaking abilities.	He **didn't get** picked for his speaking abilities.
• In informal speech, *get* is often used instead of *be* with the passive. • Passives with *get* are most often used in the simple present and the simple past tenses. • *Do/does* and *did/didn't* are used to form negative passives with *get*.	

D. Rewrite each sentence using the form of *get* + past participle.

1. The city council was chosen last month.

   The city council got chosen last month.

2. The president is elected every four years.

   _____

3. Our current president was elected two years ago.

   _____

4. Elected officials are voted in by the people.

   _____

5. They were nominated by their political party.

   _____

6. The mayor wasn't reelected.

   _____

7. The ballots aren't counted by candidates, but by volunteers.

   _____

8. Then, the winner is announced.

   _____

9. The political process was created by our founding fathers.

   _____

E. **Complete each sentence with the correct form of *get* + the past participle of the verb indicated.**

1. (past: elect) Linh Tran _____ got elected _____ mayor last month.

2. (past: choose) She _____ over Geraldo Alvelo.

3. (present: make) A lot of decisions _____ by the city council.

4. (present: clean) City streets _____ every Wednesday.

5. (present: not / clean) The beach _____ up until June.

6. (past: lower) The tuition at the community college _____.

7. (past: help) The homeless _____ in many ways.

8. (past: not / forget) Education issues _____.

9. (present: spend) Tax dollars _____ wisely.

10. (past: not / hire) A lot of new people _____.

11. (past: build) A new high school _____.

F. **Write sentences using the information given.**

1. (the President / negative present: summon / for jury duty)

   The President doesn't get summoned for jury duty. _____

2. (our mayor / past: elect / for a second term)

   _____

3. (the treasurer / past: fire / for stealing money)

   _____

4. (the judge / negative past: appoint / again)

   _____

5. (money / present: donate / by the political party)

   _____

G. **Write sentences about the elected officials in your country, state, and city using *get*.**

1. _____

2. _____

3. _____

4. _____

LESSON ⑤ What's your platform?

GOAL ■ Write and give a speech

A. Imagine that you are running for mayor. What would you do in your community? Complete each sentence.

My Platform

1. I would build more _____.

2. I would raise money for _____.

3. I would change the _____.

4. I would reorganize _____.

5. I would lower fees for _____.

6. I would fix the _____.

7. I would find a way to help _____.

8. I would convince the _____ to _____.

B. Write a short speech to convince the citizens of your community to vote for you.

_____

_____

_____

_____

_____

C. Study the chart.

Passive Modals in the Present		
	Example	
Statement	Schools **should be** built. Children **must be** protected.	Taxes **need to be** increased. Parents **have to be** involved.
Yes/No question	**Should** schools be built? **Must** children be protected?	**Do** taxes **need to** be increased? **Do** parents **have to** be involved?
Wh- question	Why **should** schools be built? How **must** children be protected?	When **do** taxes **need to** be increased? Why **do** parents **have to** be involved?

D. Find the mistake in the underlined words. Then, rewrite each sentence correctly.

1. <u>Do voters should be </u>registered?

   Should voters be registered?

2. Nomination papers <u>have to be file</u> by candidates.

   _____

3. Should less money <u>to be spent</u> on elections?

   _____

4. <u>Does candidates have to </u>be nominated for a position?

   _____

5. All citizens <u>must be encouraging</u> to participate in elections.

   _____

6. <u>Why public transportation</u> need to be improved?

   _____

7. All problems in the city <u>should identified</u>.

   _____

8. <u>How do must</u> tax dollars be spent?

   _____

9. Many changes <u>need be implemented</u> in our community.

   _____

E. **Rewrite each active statement or question using a passive modal.**

1. He should give speeches on how to help our youth.

   Speeches should be given on how to help our youth.

2. We must protect our children.

   _____

3. We should take care of our environment.

   _____

4. Should we build more parks?

   _____

5. They should raise money for a new high school.

   _____

6. Must we find a new way to communicate with our political leaders?

   _____

7. She must recruit more volunteers if she wants to get the project done.

   _____

F. **Look back at your platform in Exercise A. Rewrite your ideas using passive modals.**

1. *More housing should be built.*

2. _____

3. _____

4. _____

5. _____

6. _____

7. _____

8. _____

9. _____

PRACTICE TEST

A. Read the chart and choose the best answer.

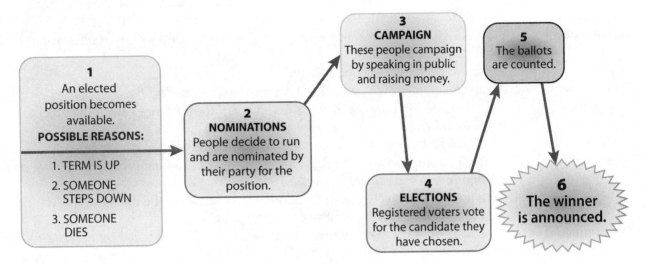

1. What is the first step in the electoral process?

   a. Someone dies.

   c. An elected position becomes available.

   b. The term is up.

   d. Someone steps down.

2. How do candidates campaign?

   a. by speaking in public

   c. both a and b

   b. by raising money

   d. neither a nor b

3. Who votes in elections?

   a. everyone

   c. registered voters

   b. registered candidates

   d. ballots

4. What is the final step in the electoral process?

   a. The candidate is chosen.

   c. The ballots are counted.

   b. The winner is announced.

   d. none of the above

GLOSSARY OF GRAMMAR TERMS

adjective	a word that describes a noun (Example: The _red_ hat)
adverb	a word that modifies a verb, adjective, or another adverb (Example: She _eats quickly_.)
affirmative	not negative and not a question (Example: _I like him_.)
apostrophe	a punctuation mark that shows missing letters in contractions or possession (Example: _It's_ or _Jim's_)
article	words used before a noun (Example: _a_, _an_, _the_)
base form	the main form of the verb, used without to (Example: _be_, _have_, _study_)
causative	a verb form that indicates that the subject of the sentence causes the object to do something. (Example: I _made_ her study.)
clause	a group of words that has a subject and a verb. (Example: _We live here_.)
comma	the punctuation mark used to indicate a pause or separation (Example: _I live in an apartment, and you live in a house._)
comparative	a form of an adjective, adverb, or noun that expresses the difference between two or more things (Example: _My sister is _taller_ than you._)
complement	a word or words that add to or complete an idea after the verb (Example: He is _happy_.)
conditional, contrary-to-fact	a structure used for talking about an imaginary situation that is not true at the present time (Example: _If I won_ the lottery, _I would buy_ a mansion.)
conditional, future	a structure used for talking about possibilities in the future (Example: _If it rains, I will bring_ an umbrella.)
conjugation	the forms of a verb (Example: I _am_, You _are_, We _are_, They _are_, He _is_, She _is_, It _is_)
conjunction	a type of word that joins other words or phrases (Example: Maria _and_ Gilberto)
consonant	any letter of the alphabet that is not a vowel (Example: b, c, d, f...)
contraction	shortening of a word, syllable, or word group by omission of a sound or letter (Example: It is = _It's_, does not = _doesn't_)
count nouns	nouns that can be counted by number (Example: one _apple_, two _apples_)
definite article	use of the when a noun is known to speaker (Example: I know _the_ store.)
direct speech	a quotation of a speaker's exact words (Example: He said, _"I am sick."_)
embedded question	a question placed within another question or a statement (Example: _Do you know when the bank opens?_)
formal	polite or respectful language (Example: _Could_ you _please_ give me that?)
future tense	a verb form in the future tense (Example: I _will study_ at that school next year.)
gerund	an -ing form of a verb that functions as a noun (Example: _Swimming_ is fun.)
imperative	a command form of a verb (Example: _Listen!_ or _Look out!_)
indefinite article	_a_ or _an_ used before a noun when _the_ is too specific (Example: There's _a_ new _restaurant_ in town.)
indirect speech	a form of a sentence that reports on what was said or written by another person (Example: _He said he was sick._)
infinitive	the main form of a verb, usually used with to (Example: I like _to run_ fast.)
informal	friendly or casual language (Example: _Can I have that?_)
irregular verb	a verb different from regular form verbs (Example: be = _am_, _are_, _is_, _was_, _were_, _being_)
modal auxiliary	a verb that indicates a mood (ability, possibility, etc.) and is followed by the base form of another verb (Example: I _can read_ English well.)
modifier	a word or phrase that describes another (Example: a _good_ friend)
negative	the opposite of affirmative (Example: She _does not_ like meat.)
noncount nouns	nouns impossible or difficult to count (Example: _water_, _love_, _rice_, _fire_)
noun	a name of a person, place, or thing (Example: _Joe_, _England_, _bottle_)

object, direct	the focus of a verb's action (Example: I eat <u>oranges</u>.)
object pronoun	replaces the noun taking the action (Example: *Julia* is nice. I like <u>her</u>.)
passive voice	a sentence structure in which the subject of the sentence receives rather than performs the action (Example: *The window <u>was opened</u>.*)
past continuous	a verb form that expresses an action in progress at a specific time in the past (Example: *I <u>was reading</u> a book at 8:00 last night.*)
past perfect	a verb form used to express an action in the past that happened before another action in the past (Example: *I <u>had</u> already <u>eaten</u> when he invited me out to dinner.*)
past tense	a verb form used to express an action or a state in the past (Example: *You <u>worked</u> yesterday.*)
period	a punctuation mark of a dot ending a sentence (.)
phrasal verb	a verb consisting of a verb plus an adverb or preposition(s), that has a meaning different from the words it is made up of (Example: <u>call up</u>, <u>write down</u>, <u>run out of</u>)
plural	indicating more than one (Example: *pencil<u>s</u>, child<u>ren</u>*)
possessive adjective	an adjective expressing possession (Example: <u>our</u> *cat*)
possessive pronoun	a word that takes the place of a noun and expresses ownership (Example: The *hat* is <u>mine</u>.)
preposition	a word that indicates relationship between objects (Example: The *pen* is <u>on</u> the *desk*.)
present perfect	a verb form that expresses a connection between the past and the present (Examples: *I <u>have lived</u> in Paris. She <u>has worked</u> here for three years.*)
present perfect continuous	a verb form that focuses on the duration of an action that began in the past and continues to the present. (Example: *I <u>have been waiting</u> in line for an hour.*)
present tense	a verb tense representing the current time, (Example: *They <u>are</u> at home right now.*)
pronoun	a word used in place of a noun (Example: *Ted* is 65. <u>He</u> is retired.)
question form	a structure that asks for an answer (Example: <u>Where is my book?</u>)
regular verb	verb with endings that are regular and follow the rule (Example: work = *work, works, worked, work<u>ing</u>*)
reporting verb	a verb used to express what has been said or written (Example: She <u>said</u> that she was leaving.)
sentence	a thought expressed in words, with a subject and verb (Example: <u>Julia works hard</u>.)
short answer	a response to a Yes/No question (Example: <u>Yes, I am.</u> <u>No he doesn't.</u>)
singular	one object (Example: <u>a cat</u>)
statement	a sentence (Example: <u>The weather is rainy today</u>.)
subject	the noun that does the action in a sentence (Example: <u>The gardener</u> works here.)
subject pronoun	a pronoun that takes the place of a subject (Example: *John* is a student. <u>He</u> is smart.)
superlative	a form of an adjective that expresses the highest degree of something (Example: <u>happiest</u>, <u>most beautiful</u>)
syllable	a part of a word as determined by vowel sounds and rhythm (Example: ta-*ble*)
tag question	a short informal question at the end of a sentence (Example: *You like soup, <u>don't you?</u>*)
tense	the part of a verb that shows the past, present, or future time (Example: He *talk<u>ed</u>*.)
verb	word describing an action or state (Example: The boys <u>walk</u> to school. I <u>am</u> tired.)
vowels	the letters *a, e, i, o, u*, and sometimes *y*
***Wh*- question**	a question that asks for information, usually starting with *Who, What, When, Where,* or *Why*. (Example: <u>Where</u> do you live?) *How* is often included in this group.
***Yes/No* question**	a question that asks for an affirmative or a negative answer (Example: <u>Are you happy?</u>)

GRAMMAR REFERENCE

Used to in Affirmative and Negative Statements	
Example	**Rule**
Diego *used to* <u>study</u> by himself. He *used to* <u>take</u> English classes.	**Affirmative:** *used to* + base verb
Diego *did not use to* <u>study</u> with friends. He *didn't use to* <u>exercise</u> at night.	**Negative:** *did* + *not (didn't)* + *use to* + base verb **Incorrect:** ~~I didn't used to go to school.~~
Use *used to* + *base verb* to talk about a past habit or custom that was true for a period of time in the past, but is not true now.	

Use to and *Used to* in *Yes/No* and *Wh-* Questions		
	Example	**Rule**
***Yes/No* Questions**	**Did** Minh **use to** work? **Did** Bita **use to** study English?	***Yes/No* Question:** *did* + subject + *use to* + base verb
***Wh-* Questions** **(where, when, why)**	Where **did** Minh **use to** work? When **did** Bita **use to** study? Why **did** Minh **use to** make jewelry?	***Wh-* Question:** *Wh-* word + *did* + subject + *use to* + base verb
***Wh-* Questions** **(who, what)**	Who **used to** live in Iran? What **did** Minh **use to** do in Vietnam?	***Wh-* Question:** *Wh-* word + *did* + subject + *use to* + base verb
• Most *yes/no* and *wh-* questions omit the *-d* in *used to*. • When *who* asks about the subject, the *-d* should not be omitted.		

Used to vs. *Be used to*	
Example	**Rule**
I **used to** work part time.	*Used to* + base verb is used to talk about a past habit or custom.

<u>With gerund:</u>
   Rosa **is used to** managing her time.
<u>With noun phrase:</u>
   She **is used to** realistic goals.
	Be used to + gerund or noun phrase means *be accustomed to*. It shows what is normal for someone.

• Omit the *-d* in the negative of *used to*.
   I didn't **use to** eat junk food.
• Do not omit the *-d* in the negative of *be used to*.
   We **aren't used to** working late.	

Contrary-to-Fact Conditionals: Statements

Condition (*if* + subject + past tense verb)	Result (subject + *would* + base verb)
If I had a million dollars, **If you didn't have** so much work, **If she were** a smart consumer, **If I weren't** busy,	**I would buy** a new house. **you would take** a long vacation. **she would read** sales ads carefully. **I would shop** around.

- A contrary-to-fact statement is a sentence that is not true at this point in time.
- A comma is used between the two clauses when the *if*-clause comes first.
- The *if*-clause can come first or second. When it comes second, no comma is used.
    I would buy a new house **if I had** a million dollars.
- In the *if*-clause, use *were* instead of *was* with *I, he, she,* and *it*.

Contrary-to-Fact Conditionals: *Yes/No* Questions

if + subject + past tense / *would* + subject + base verb	Short answer	
If you had more money, **would you buy** a car? **If he didn't have** so much work, **would he take** a vacation? **If they weren't** busy, **would they shop** around?	Yes, I **would**. Yes, he **would**. Yes, they **would**.	No, I **wouldn't**. No, he **wouldn't**. No, they **wouldn't**.

- A *Yes/No* question in a contrary-to-fact conditional is formed in the result clause.
- The *if*-clause can come first or second. When it comes second, no comma is used.
    Would you buy a car **if you had** more money?

Contrary-to-Fact Conditionals: *Wh-* Questions

Question	Answer
If + subject + past tense, *wh-* word + *would* + subject +base verb	Subject + *would* + base verb
If you received a bad meal, what would you do?	I would speak to the manager.
If a clerk yelled at him, how would he react?	He would calmly walk out of the store.
If her computer stopped working, whom would she call?	She would call the store where she bought it.

- A *wh-* question in a contrary-to-fact conditional is formed in the result clause.
- The *if*-clauses can come first or second. When it comes second, no comma is used.
    What would you do **if you received** a bad meal?

Future Conditionals

Condition (*if* + subject + present tense verb)	Result (subject + *will* + base verb)
If you open an account, **If she saves** enough money, **If the accountant is** in the office tomorrow,	**you will receive** free checking. **she will buy** a house. **he will do** our taxes.

- A future conditional sentence tells about something that may happen in the future.
- The *if*-clause can come first or second. When the *if*-clause comes first, a comma is used between the two clauses. When it comes second, no comma is used.
    I will open an account **if the rates are** good.

Comparative and Superlative Adjectives

Type of adjective	Simple form	Comparative form	Superlative form
One-syllable adjectives	cheap	**cheaper**	**the cheapest**
One-syllable adjectives that end in -e	safe	**safer**	**the safest**
One-syllable adjectives that end in *consonant-vowel-consonant*	big	**bigger**	**the biggest**
Two-syllable adjectives that end in -y	cozy	**cozier**	**the coziest**
Other two-syllable adjectives	recent	**more recent**	**the most recent**
Some two-syllable adjectives have two forms	quiet	**quieter** or **more quiet**	**the quietest** or **the most quiet**
	friendly	**friendlier** or **more friendly**	**the friendliest** or **the most friendly**
Adjectives with three or more syllables	expensive	**more expensive**	**the most expensive**

- Use the comparative form to compare two things.
- If the second item is expressed, use *than*.
    New York is **bigger than** Los Angeles.
- Use the superlative form to compare one thing to two or more things.
- A prepositional phrase is sometimes used at the end of a superlative sentence.
    My town is the friendliest town **in the world.**

Comparative and Superlative Questions

Question word	Subject	Verb	Adjective (+ noun)	Rule
Which	one area	**is**	**bigger?** **the safest?**	Use *be* when following with an adjective.
Which		**has**	**more rooms?** **the biggest floor plan?**	Use *have* before an adjective + noun.

Question	Short answer	Long answer	Rule
Which one **is bigger,** the condominium or the house?	The condominium.	The condominium **is bigger than** the house. The condominium **is bigger.**	When talking about two things, and mentioning both of them, use *than*.
Which place **has more rooms,** the condominium or the house?	The house.	The house **has more rooms than** the condominium. The house **has more rooms.**	When talking about two things, but only mentioning one of them, do not use *than*.

Irregular Comparative and Superlative Adjectives

	Simple form	Comparative form	Superlative form
Irregular adjectives	good bad far little much/many	**better** **worse** **farther** **less** **more**	**the best** **the worst** **the farthest** **the least** **the most**
Irregular adverbs	well badly a little a lot	**better** **worse** **less** **more**	**the best** **the worst** **the least** **the most**

Compound Adjectives

Example	Rule
I want to buy a **three-bedroom** house.	number + noun
Kenji is a **foreign-born** citizen.	adjective + past participle
We placed a **full-price** offer on the house.	adjective + noun

- Compound adjectives are two words used together to modify a noun.
- Use a hyphen between the words in a compound adjective.

As many . . . as / As much . . . as

Example	Rule
This house has **as many** bedrooms **as** the other one.	To show that two count nouns are equal or not equal in quantity, use *as many* + count noun + *as*.
My agent doesn't have **as much** time for me **as** I would like.	To show that two noncount nouns are equal or not equal in quantity, use *as much* + noncount noun + *as*.

Embedded Questions: *Wh*- Questions

Wh-question	Introductory question	Embedded question
Where is Orange Avenue?	Can you show me	**where** Orange Avenue **is**?
When does the library **open**?	Do you know	**when** the library **opens**?

- An embedded question is a question that is placed within another question or statement.
- Use an embedded question to make a question more polite.
- In an embedded *wh*- question, the subject comes before the verb.
- The auxiliaries *do/does* are not used in embedded questions.

Embedded Questions: *Yes/No* Questions

Yes/No question	Introductory question	Embedded question
Is the library near here?	Can you tell me	**if** the library **is** near here?
Does the pool **open** at 8:00?	Do you know	**if** the pool **opens** at 8:00?
Does the museum **close** at 9:00?	Do you remember	**if** the museum **closes** at 9:00?

- For *yes/no* questions, use *if* before the embedded question.
- In embedded *yes/no* questions, the subject usually comes before the verb. One exception is embedded *yes/no* questions with *there is/there are*.
    Can you tell me if *there is* a bank in this neighborhood?
- The auxiliaries *do/does* are not used in embedded questions.

Embedded Questions in Statements

Question	Statement	Embedded question
_Wh-_ Question **Where** can he **sign up** for baseball? **When does** the shoe store **open**?	I'm not sure I have no idea	**where** he can **sign up** for baseball. **when** the shoe store **opens**.
Yes/No Question **Are there** books on tape in the library? **Does** he **use** a computer?	Please tell me I wonder	**if there are** books on tape in the library. **if** he **uses** a computer.

- The auxiliaries *do/does* are not used in embedded questions.
- For *yes/no* questions, use *if* before the embedded question.
- In embedded questions, the subject usually comes before the verb. One exception is embedded *yes/no* questions with *there is/there are*.

Embedded Questions with Infinitive Phrases

Embedded question	Embedded question with infinitive phrase
He doesn't know **what he should do**.	He doesn't know **what to do**.
Please tell me **how I can find** the freeway.	Please tell me **how to find** the freeway.
We can't decide **whether (or if) we should stay**.	We can't decide **whether to stay**.

- Some embedded questions with *can, could,* and *should* can be shortened with an infinitive phrase if the subject of each clause in the sentence is the same.
- *Whether* has the same meaning as *if.* Use *whether* before an infinitive instead of *if.*
- Use an infinitive after *know how.*
  - He doesn't **know how to play** the guitar.

Present Perfect

	Subject	*Has/Have*	Past participle	
Affirmative Statement	He	**has**	**eaten**	five pieces of fruit today.
	Subject	*Has/Have*	*not/never*	**Past participle**
Negative Statement	You	**have**	**never**	**been** to a doctor.
	Has/Have	**Subject**	**Past participle**	
Yes/No Question	**Have**	you	**walked**	a lot this week?
	Wh- word	*Has/Have*	**Subject**	**Past participle**
Wh- Question	How long	**has**	he	**had** a cold?

- Use the present perfect to show that: (a) something happened at an unspecified time in the past; (b) something happened more than once in the past; (c) something started at a specific time in the past and continues in the present.

Present Perfect Continuous Statements					
	Subject	*Has/Have*	*Been*	Present participle	
Affirmative Statement	I	have	been	walking	30 minutes a day for the past month.
	I	have	been	exercising	for an hour.
	Subject	*Has/Have not*	*Been*	Present participle	
Negative Statement	He	hasn't	been	eating	healthy food lately.
	You	haven't	been	sleeping	enough recently.

- The present perfect continuous emphasizes the duration of an activity or state that started in the past and continues in the present. It also shows that an activity has been in progress recently.
- With some verbs (*work, live, teach*), there is no difference in meaning between the present perfect and the present perfect continuous: I *have lived/have been living* here since 2000.
- Some verbs are not usually used in the continuous form: *be, believe, hate, have, known, like, want.*

Present Perfect Continuous Questions					
	Has/Have	Subject	*Been*	Present participle	
Yes/No Question	Has Have Have	he you they	been been been	**researching** **contacting** **filling out**	insurance companies lately? insurance agents? their health history forms?
	Wh-word	*Has/Have*	Subject	*Been*	Present participle
Wh- Question	How long How long How long	have has has	they he she	been	**thinking** about insurance? **looking** for a new insurance company? **fighting** that claim?

Past Perfect Tense: Forms					
	Subject	*Had/Hadn't*	Past participle	Complement	
Statement	I I	had hadn't	sent received	my resume by last month. a response before today.	
	Wh- word	*Had/Hadn't*	Subject	Past participle	Complement
Question	Why	had had	she you	had hired	an interview before? him?

- The past perfect tense is formed with *had/had not* (*hadn't*) + past participle.
- Subject pronouns (except *it*) can contract with *had*: *I'd, you'd, he'd, she'd, we'd, they'd.*

Past Perfect Tense: Uses	
Example	**Rule**
Before I got my job as a computer technician, I **had worked** as a delivery person.	To show that an event happened before another event in the past.
She **had** already **prepared** her resume **when** the company called her for an interview.	To show that an event happened before the verb in the *when* clause.
After I **had written** my resume and cover letter, I realized it was too late to send it.	With *after*, to show that something was finished before another event in the past.
There were a lot of job applicants **because** the company **had posted** the position on the Internet.	After *because*, to show a prior reason.
Many of the employees **had never worked** in sales **before** this job.	With *never . . . before*, in relation to a past event.
My supervisor thanked me for all the hard work **that** I **had done**.	In a *who/that/which* clause to show a past event.

Past Perfect Tense with Simple Past	
Example	**Explanation**
Before Ranjit **got** the job as a repairperson, (simple past) he **had worked** as an assembler. (past perfect)	Use the past perfect for the event that happened first in the past.
When she **arrived** at the interview, (simple past) the interviewer **had** already **read** her resume. (past perfect)	Use the simple past for the event that happened second.

```
                                                now
                                                 |
past ◄--------------↑------------------------↑---|-------► future
     1. Ranjit had worked         Ranjit got the job
     2. The interviewer had read  she arrived
```

Indirect Speech	
Direct speech	**Indirect speech**
"The most important thing **is** your health."	The doctor **said** (that) the most important thing **was** my health.
"You **eat** too much sugar."	The doctor **told me** (that) I **ate** too much sugar.

- Indirect speech reports on what someone has said.
- The use of *that* is optional in indirect speech.
- In indirect speech, you *say* something or you *tell* someone something.
- *Tell* is usually followed by an indirect object noun or pronoun.
- Other verbs like *say* are: *agree, announce, answer, complain, explain, reply, state.*
- Other verbs like *tell* are: *assure, advise, convince, notify, promise, remind, teach, warn.*
- Change the present tense in direct speech to the past tense in indirect speech.
- Change the pronouns to reflect the correct person.

Indirect Questions

	Direct question	Indirect question
Wh-Question	He asked, "**Where is** the campground?" They asked, "**How far are** you **going**?"	He asked **where** the campground **was**. They asked **how far** you **were going**.
Yes/No Question	You asked, "**Are** we **stopping** now?" We asked, "**Did** you **see** the rest stop?"	You asked **if** we **were stopping** now. We asked **if** you **had seen** the rest stop.

- An indirect question reports on what someone asked.
- Use statement word order in an indirect question. Use a period at the end.
- For *yes/no* questions, use *if* before the subject.
- Follow this sequence of tenses:

Direct Question	Indirect Question
simple present	simple past
present continuous	past continuous
simple past	past perfect

Indirect Speech: Modals

Direct Speech	Indirect Speech
He said, "I can read nutrition labels."	He said (that) he could read nutrition labels.
She said, "You may need some fiber." (may=possibility)	She said (that) I might need some fiber.
The doctor said, "You may start eating more fat." (may=permission)	The doctor said (that) I could start eating more fat.
I said, "I must stop eating so much sugar."	I said (that) I had to stop eating so much sugar."
They said, "We will start paying more attention to what we eat."	They said (that) they would start paying more attention to what they ate.

- The modal *should* does not change form in indirect speech.
     He said, "You should eat more fruit." He said (that) I should eat more fruit.

Indirect Speech: Sequence of Tenses

Direct speech	Indirect speech
He said, "I **sleep** eight hours a night." (present)	He said (that) he **slept** eight hours a night. (simple past)
She said, "I **am going** to exercise today." (present continuous)	She said (that) she **was going** to exercise that day. (past continuous)
He said, "You **ate** too much yesterday." (simple past)	He said (that) I **had eaten** too much the day before. (past perfect)

- In talking about a general truth, the sequence of tenses is often not applied.
     The doctor said aspirin **is** a non-prescription medicine.
- Time words change in indirect speech: **today** → **that day; yesterday** → **the day before; tomorrow** → **the next** (or **following**) **day; this morning** → **that morning.**

Adjective Clauses

Person	The teacher **who** influenced me the most in my life is Mrs. Hargrove.
	(The teacher is Mrs. Hargrove. **She** influenced me the most in my life.)
Place	She taught at the school **where** my brother went.
	(She taught at the school. My brother went **there**.)
Thing	Mrs. Hargrove gave me a book **that** always reminds me of her.
	(Mrs. Hargrove gave me a book. **It** always reminds me of her.)

- An adjective clause is a group of words that describe the preceding noun (either a subject noun or an object noun.)
- *Who, where,* and *that* are relative pronouns that begin adjective clauses. Relative pronouns replace the subject or object. (See bold words above.)
- All adjective clauses contain a noun and a verb and express an incomplete thought.

Restrictive Adjective Clauses

Main clause	Restrictive adjective clause
A homemaker is a person	**who takes care of a home and a family.**
The job	**(that) I really want** is in Texas.

- Restrictive adjective clauses give essential information about the noun they refer to. They cannot be omitted without losing the meaning of the sentence.
- A relative pronoun (*that, which, who[m], whose, when, where*) that is the object of the adjective clause can be omitted.

Non-Restrictive Adjective Clauses

Main clause	Non-restrictive adjective clause	
My brother-in-law,	**who owns his own business,**	works very hard.
I quit my job,	**which I never really liked anyway.**	

- Non-restrictive adjective clauses give extra non-essential information about the noun they refer to. They can be omitted without changing the sense of the sentence.
- Commas are used to set off the non-restrictive adjective clause from the main clause.
- The relative pronoun cannot be omitted from non-restrictive adjective clauses.
- The relative pronoun *that* is not used in non-restrictive adjective clauses.

Omission of the Relative Pronoun in Adjective Clauses

The relative pronoun can be omitted from the adjective clause if there is a <u>subject</u> following the **relative pronoun.** Look at the examples below:

The book (**that**) <u>she</u> gave to me sits on the shelf above my desk.

She is the teacher (**who*/whom**) <u>I</u> told you about.

She is the first teacher (**that**) <u>I</u> had when I came here.

I'm sure (**that**) <u>she</u> knows how hard you worked.

Note that the relative pronoun cannot be omitted in the following sentences because there is no subject following the relative pronoun. (Therefore, the relative pronoun IS the subject.)

Is she the teacher who gave you the book?

I want to get her something that will remind her how important she is.

*Who is more common in everyday conversation. *Whom* is used in more formal situations.

Passive Voice: Form					
	Subject	*Be*	**Past participle**	*by* + person/thing	
Statement	A meeting	**is**	**held**		every day.
	The orders	**were**	**sent**	by Jim	yesterday.
	Be	**Subject**	**Past participle**	*by* + person/thing	
***Yes/No* Question**	**Is**	a meeting	**held**		every day?
	Were	the orders	**sent**	by Jim	yesterday?

- Use the passive voice to emphasize the object of the action or when the doer of the action is unknown or unimportant.
- Use the passive with *by* if the doer of the action is mentioned.

Passive Voice: Overview of Tenses	
Tense	**Passive (*be* + past participle)**
Simple Present	The decision **is made**.
Present Continuous	The decision **is being made**.
Future	The decision **will be made**. / The decision **is going to be made**.
Simple Past	The decision **was made**.
Past Continuous	The decision **was being made**.
Present Perfect	The decision **has been made**.
Past Perfect	The decision **had been made**.

- In the passive voice, the past participle is the same for all tenses. Only the form of *be* changes.
- An adverb can be placed between the auxiliary verb and the past participle.
     The decision was *already* made.

Passives with *Get*	
Passive with *be*	**Passive with *get***
Government officials **are elected** by the people.	Government officials **get elected** by the people.
They **aren't** voted in by their peers.	They **don't get** voted in by their peers.
The mayor **was chosen** for his environmental agenda.	The mayor **got chosen** for his environmental agenda.
He **wasn't picked** for his speaking abilities.	He **didn't get** picked for his speaking abilities.

- In informal speech, *get* is often used instead of *be* with the passive.
- Passives with *get* are most often used in the simple present and the simple past tenses.
- *Do/does* and *did/didn't* are used to form negative passives with *get*.

Passive Modals in the Present and Past

Present	Past
New laws **can be** written.	New laws **could have been** written.
New laws **may be** written.	New laws **may have been** written.
New laws **might be** written.	New laws **might have been** written.
New laws **would be** written.	New laws **would have been** written.

- *Can* is the only modal with a different past form: *could*.
- Passive modals can be used in past tense *yes/no* and *wh-* questions.
    - **Might** a new park **have been** built?
    - When **could** we **have registered** to vote?

Causative Verbs

Example	Explanation
The government **makes you register** and **insure** your car. The court **makes you fill out** a jury summons.	**Make** means *force* or *require*.
The police **let you drive** in the carpool lane if you have more than one person in your car. The court **lets you opt out** of jury duty if you have small children to care for.	**Let** means *permit*.
The DMV **has you take** a written test before you get your license. Some courts **have you call** in before you report for jury service.	**Have** means *give a job or task to someone*.

- *Make, let*, and *have* are called causative verbs because one person causes or allows another to do something.
- The sentence structure is: *causative verb + object + base form*.

Gerunds and Infinitives as Subjects

Example	Explanation
Investing time in our community problems is important. **Finding** solutions as a community is key. **Raising** money isn't easy.	A gerund can be the subject of a sentence.
It is important **to invest** time in our community problems. It is key **to find** solutions as a community. It isn't easy **to raise** money.	An infinitive phrase can be the subject of a sentence. An infinitive phrase is often used with *it* as the subject of a sentence. The meaning is the same as using a gerund subject.

- Gerund and infinitive subjects are followed by a singular verb.

Can, Could, and Should

Example	Rule
You **can** eat at the Mexican restaurant. We **could** go to the bookstore.	*Can* and *could* are used to offer a suggestion when there is more than one choice.
They **should** go to the library today. You **shouldn't** be late for your class.	*Should/shouldn't* is used when there is a recommended choice.

- *Can* and *could* have the same meaning when making suggestions.
- *Could* does not have a past meaning in this case.

Verbs with Two Objects

Example	Explanation
My boss gave **me a promotion**. I gave **Tito the mail**.	Many verbs can have both a direct object and an indirect object.
The cashier gave the receipt **to me**. Sam bought a computer **for her**.	When the indirect object comes last, the preposition **to** or **for** is usually used.
I sent **Ana the e-mail**. *or* I sent **the e-mail to Ana**.	With many verbs, either the direct or the indirect object can come first.
Can you **explain the plan to me**? ~~Can you **explain me the plan**?~~	With the verbs **say, describe, suggest,** and **explain**, the indirect object *cannot* come first.
A package was given to Chan. **Chan was given** a package.	With passive sentences with two objects, two structures are possible.

- **To** is used with *bring, give, lend, offer, pay, read, sell, send, show, take, teach, tell, write.*
- **For** is used with *build, buy, do, find, get, make, prepare.*
- No preposition is used with *ask, cost, wish.*

Two-Word Phrasal Verbs

Example	Explanation
She **turned on** the copier.	Two-word phrasal verbs consist of verb + preposition.
She **turned** the copier **on**. She **turned** it **on**.	Some phrasal verbs can be separated by a noun or pronoun. If a pronoun is used, it must separate the parts of the verb.
Let's **forget about** it.	Some phrasal verbs cannot be separated. These phrasal verbs can be followed by a pronoun.

- Some two-word phrasal verbs that can be separated: *act out, call in/up, fill out, leave out, put on, set up, turn on, write down.*
- Some two-word phrasal verbs that cannot be separated: *ask for, focus on, forget about, knock on, look into, pay for, plan on, succeed in, talk to/about.*

Tag Questions with Indefinite Compound Pronouns and Negative Words

Example	Explanation
Everyone is getting a raise, aren't **they**? **Somebody** is sick, aren't **they**?	In tag questions, use *they* to refer to *everyone, everybody, someone, somebody, nobody,* and *no one*.
Nobody has come in late, **have they**?	Use an affirmative tag with *nothing, nobody,* and *no one*.
She has **hardly** had time, **has she**?	Use an affirmative tag with *never, hardly,* and *scarcely*.
Nothing is going to happen, is **it**?	Use *it* in tag questions that refer to *nothing*.

Tag Questions

Tense	Affirmative statement	Negative tag question	Answer
Simple Present	You work,	**don't** you?	Yes, I do. No, I don't.
Present Continuous	You are working,	**aren't** you?	Yes, I am. No, I'm not.
Future	You will work,	**won't** you?	Yes, I will. No, I won't.
Simple Past	They talked,	**didn't** they?	Yes, they did. No, they didn't.
Past Continuous	They were talking,	**weren't** they?	Yes, they were. No, they weren't.
Present Perfect	They have talked,	**haven't** they?	Yes, they have. No, they haven't.
Past Perfect	They had talked,	**hadn't** they?	Yes, they had. No, they hadn't.

- Tag questions are used to check if something is true or to ask for agreement.
- A tag question uses an auxiliary verb + a subject pronoun.
- The tag question uses the same tense as the main verb.
- A tag question can consist of a negative tag statement and an affirmative tag question.
    You aren't a new employee, *are* you?
    She won't apply for the job, *will* she?
- Negative tags are usually contracted.

Should and Should have

Should	Should have
You **should analyze** your financial situation before getting a mortgage.	You **should have analyzed** your financial situation before getting a mortgage.
She **shouldn't buy** a house in that neighborhood.	She **shouldn't have bought** a house in that neighborhood.
Should we **use** a realtor?	**Should** we **have used** a realtor?
Where **should** we **keep** our financial documents?	Where **should** we **have kept** our financial documents?

- To give or ask for advice about a present situation, use *should* + base verb.
- To express regret about a past situation, use *should have* + past participle.

PHOTO CREDITS

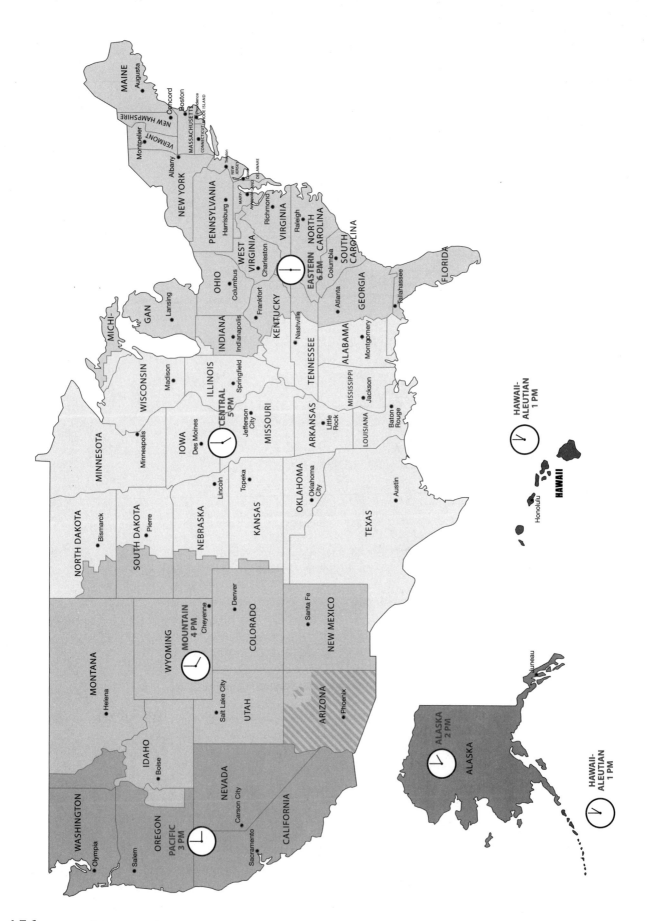